The Infinite Game

The Infinite Game

How to live well together

Niki Harré

AUCKLAND
UNIVERSITY
PRESS

To my father, John Harré

First published 2018
Auckland University Press
University of Auckland
Private Bag 92019
Auckland 1142
New Zealand
www.press.auckland.ac.nz

© Niki Harré, 2018

ISBN 978 1 86940 878 7

Published with the assistance of Creative New Zealand

ARTS COUNCIL OF NEW ZEALAND TOI AOTEAROA

A catalogue record for this book is available from
the National Library of New Zealand

Book design by Katrina Duncan
Typesetting and layout by WordsAlive Ltd
Cover design by Kalee Jackson

This book was printed on FSC® Certified Paper

Printed in Singapore by Markono Print Media Pte Ltd

Contents

PART TWO – THE INFINITE PLAYER

Welcome to the Infinite Game

Welcome to the infinite game. The infinite game is a game about our times, a game about how to live well together. Everyone is invited. We don't *need* you exactly, but whatever you offer will make the game a little better for the rest of us. With a bit of luck, you'll get something out of it too.

Like any game, the infinite game works best if the players appear to take it seriously. This means that if you want to play, you are asked to concentrate, to try hard, and to act as if it matters. In the end, it does not matter. But if everyone pretends there is some goal, something worth striving towards, it will be a better game. So let's get started.

—o—o—o—

In 1986 the philosopher James P. Carse wrote that in life there are at least two kinds of games: finite games and the infinite game. He described these games in a book called *Finite and Infinite Games: A Vision of Life as Play and Possibility*.[1] I've taken some key insights from his book, played with them a little (or a lot), and added some contributions of my own. The characteristics of these games are laid out as a list of fifteen paired features on the following page.

Features of the infinite game and finite games

1. The purpose of the infinite game is to continue the play
    The purpose of a finite game is to win
2. The infinite game is played with that which we value for its own sake
    Finite games are played with the values relevant to the game
3. The infinite game includes finite games
    Finite games may exist outside the infinite game
4. The infinite game invites others in
    Finite games include only select people
5. Infinite players relate to the humanity in each other
    In finite games others are allies, pawns, spectators or competitors
6. The infinite game values open-ended expression
    Finite games value expression only within the mediums and rules set by the game
7. The infinite game may provide a deep sense of connection with others
    In finite games victory may be joyful but must be guarded
8. Infinite players may come and go
    Finite players must be alert – to relax is dangerous
9. The infinite game is an open network in which everything is interconnected
    Finite games are discrete entities that may expand or replicate
10. The infinite game tends towards diversity
    Finite games tend towards sameness
11. Infinite players are in awe of life in all its forms
    Finite players attempt to control the life forms relevant to the game
12. The infinite game seeks and responds to information about the world
    Winners of finite games claim knowledge of the world which may be treated as the truth
13. Infinite players attempt to understand themselves
    Finite players attempt to train themselves
14. The infinite game looks to the future and does not assume the past will reoccur
    In finite games players try to replicate the winning strategies of the past
15. The rules of the infinite game must change over time or the game will cease
    To change or break the rules of a finite game is a violation

Are you starting to get the idea? The features of the infinite game and finite games will be teased out more fully in Part One of this book. For now, to help understand the difference between these two types of games, let's imagine beach cricket as the infinite game and compare it with a finite game of international cricket. In beach cricket, someone has a tennis ball and ideally a bat of some sort, although a piece of driftwood will do. Teams are created from whoever is willing; everyone on the beach is invited to play. Age, prior experience with the game, fitness, being able to speak the language of the instigators, none of these are prerequisites to – or protections from – being encouraged to have a go: *'We'll teach you – it'll be fun!'* The rules are set, but most people can't quite remember them and make lots of mistakes. When it's a four-year-old boy's turn to hold the bat, the rules are changed completely: he doesn't actually have to *hit* the ball to run, and no one tries to get him out.

Experienced players are often theatrical, exaggerating or slowing down their movements to the laughter and spontaneous applause of others. Experienced players may also focus intensely when up against each other, trying hard to make as many runs as possible or get the opposing player out. The most valued player is not, however, the best cricketer, but the one who has the knack of making everyone feel welcome. He calls for breaks in the play to show those who are uncertain how to hold the bat and run with it to the opposing wicket. She senses when to cajole a shy player into running into the sea after the ball and when to back off and let the player leave the action to others.

People leave the game for a while, switch teams to keep the numbers more or less even, and none of this matters. It doesn't even matter when a teenager misses a great catch because she is watching a surfer catch a wave, although everyone groans loudly. The truth is, everyone is somewhat distracted by the blue of the ocean, the crunch of the sand, and the oystercatchers' attempts to crack open shellfish with their long orange beaks.

As a player, you experience moments of deep contentment, wrapped in a warm blanket of goodwill. It is as if you are in a time apart from time, a space apart from space, where no one has anything better to do than simply be together. Perhaps you feel an absurd love for this odd collection of people, whose lives you may know little or nothing about.

—∘—∘—∘—

International cricket is rather different. For starters, the teams are carefully selected. Have you ever been selected to play cricket for your country? I suspected not. And it would be ridiculous for players to switch sides or to change the rules part way through the game. How would we know which team won? Players must focus completely on the game and all are needed. Missing a great catch because you are texting your girlfriend in the stand is out of the question. And the setting, apart from the cheers and boos of the spectators, is largely irrelevant. The grass on which the game is played has been carefully cut to the right length and the pitch protected overnight to ensure it does not become sticky from unwanted rain or dew. Victory, when it comes, is euphoric for the winners and dismal for the losers. No matter how small the winning margin, the difference between the two outcomes is absolute. The post-game ritual requires the losers to concede defeat and the audience to praise the winners, usually by detailed public discussion of the brilliant plays that led to their triumph.

International cricketers learn their sport by studying the winning strategies of the past. They acquire a coach and train their bodies and minds to be the perfect cricket clone, just fractionally better than what has gone before. In fact, if I was to line up elite sportspeople in front of you and get you to guess their sport – rugby, swimming, gymnastics, middle-distance running – you would probably do very well indeed just by looking at their body shapes.

Like all master finite players, elite cricketers want to control the outcome of the game before it begins. Surprise is to be eliminated. Thus, international cricket, like other finite games, is inherently conservative. Players aim towards a known goal and follow a well-worn path to get there. By contrast, one day's game of beach cricket is never the same as another's. The players reconfigure and change the game depending on the tide, the wind and the collective mood. They may even play a different game entirely. A sand-castle city anyone? *'Come on, I'll lend you a spade!'*

—◦—◦—◦—

This book is an invitation to imagine life as an infinite game. Just like beach cricket, the infinite game thrives when people offer their talents, look out for each other, and know when to break the rules. It's a game that deals in joy – the joy of being deeply alive and trusting that others are on your side.

This book is also an invitation to take a critical look at the finite games that surround you. Sure, international cricket has its place; but are the competitive structures that underpin our major institutions (the qualification game, the economic growth game, the housing market game, the funding game, the publishing game, the career game, the patriotism game, the political election game) really the best way to draw out people's talents, create community and revitalise the natural world? How would life look if we flipped our usual perspective – if we put our finite games aside for a moment and considered instead what we really, truly value and how to keep *that* in play?

The infinite game is not an invitation to anarchy. Even beach cricket has nominal rules and boundaries. When it comes to life, we do need structure. After all, we need to grow food, build shelters, make clothes, access clean water, care for people who are ill, teach children, respond to collective threats, and much more besides. We also need challenges and goals. We may want to restore a historic building, plant fruit trees, learn how to play the guitar, or get bicycle stands installed at the local library. We may also want to be a good parent, learn to forgive all those dreadful people who have betrayed us in the hope of finally finding inner peace, or give up smoking. We may even want to discriminate between people on some dimension and acknowledge those who are particularly skilled at an activity. To do all this, we need finite games. We need boundaries, allies and rules, and to spend time learning and repeating the games of the past. I'm rather glad, for example, that my doctor has been to medical school and absorbed the rules of Western medicine.

But, over time, finite games often drift from their original purpose. They become distorted and even absurd under the pressure of human foibles. We devise tokens to facilitate exchanges between us and then develop entire industries that treat these tokens as sacred (money and the empires that surround it). We replicate popular consumer goods until every city groans with the weight of products that are identical the world over. We insist that some games, such as our national pride, are so important that they must be maintained at almost any cost. When a finite game takes *itself*, rather than its *purpose*, too seriously, we are in trouble. This would be like the experienced players in beach cricket spending every moment of their summer holiday training to beat the other players when, actually, it's not about the winning. It's not even, in fact, about the cricket. There's a bigger game in play.

—o—o—o—

Why have I written this book? I am a community psychologist at the University of Auckland in New Zealand. I have long been interested in social and environmental activism, and in 2011 I wrote a book called *Psychology for a Better World: Strategies to Inspire Sustainability*.[2] The aim of that book was to apply the most interesting and relevant ideas from psychological research to engaging people in sustainability-related issues. *Psychology for a Better World* was very much about working *with* people, which is also a core focus of the book you are reading now. This approach stands in contrast to much writing from a psychological perspective, which is about 'behaviour change'. You probably know the drill: people are failing to recycle, driving their cars too much, or eating the wrong food. If we can identify and manipulate the 'barriers' to change and 'incentives' for change, we can bring them into line. The hope is that this push, alongside technological advances and the right laws and international agreements, just might save us from the various ills we otherwise seem headed towards.

Well, changing the behaviour of other adults has always seemed to me both patronising and misguided. What we need, if we are going to promote human and ecological flourishing, is people working together on creative solutions, not experts training others like circus animals. The enormous beauty and power of our species lies in our capacity for collective innovation. It is an endless, uncertain task, improving this world of ours and trying to do so with love and joy. It takes both big, powerful players and small, discrete players each working within their sphere of influence – experimenting, adapting, and negotiating new practices; and the policies, laws and technological innovations that help hold these practices in place. We need to ignite that creative capacity in each other – not smother it with assumptions that 'we' (whoever 'we' may be) know best.

After *Psychology for a Better World* was published, I found myself giving talks and workshops to numerous groups of inspiring, struggling people full of energy and generosity. They all wanted to contribute in some way to the common good, although the focus of each varied. I met young climate-change activists, social justice-oriented school teachers, volunteers who maintain the health of their local stream, people with a ferocious love of animals who push to abolish factory farming, unionists advocating for a living wage, and eco-fashion designers.

Still, I sensed that we, as people who care about the common good, were missing something. We certainly had the issues covered. You name it, someone is working on it: climate change, child poverty, women's rights, housing insecurity, protecting native plants and animals, wealth inequality, indigenous people's loss of land. Where there is injustice and harm, you will also find people refusing, in one form or another, to accept that our current practices are good enough. There are also people demonstrating alternatives to the status quo by living in tiny houses, designing low-carbon urban transport systems, harnessing sustainable energy, farming organically, running cooperative businesses, implementing democratic decision-making, and constructing self-sufficient buildings. And there is no shortage of knowledge, energy and intelligence behind these efforts. Figuring out how to live well together is, after all, our most challenging task. It therefore attracts people who have the imagination and stamina to take on hard problems. Smart people are not all attracted to high-status, money-making positions. Really smart people – even in the conventional sense – want to be part of creating new games, not just winning the old ones.

But, it seemed to me, tackling the various issues that infuriate and inspire us isn't enough. What if we won the war on climate change? What if women led 50 per cent of the major corporations? What if we found a renewable energy source to run the entire transport system? What if the cooperative became the favoured business model? What if every farm was organic? Is the creation of the collective good life simply the sum of its parts?

I don't think so. Something must hold those parts together. Otherwise, in our rush to solve this or that problem, we pull against each other and create (sometimes horrific) collateral damage. We sacrifice yet another river to create clean energy, we support yet another military intervention to restore human rights, we get caught in destructive debates about whether jobs or an endangered species are more important, and we compete with each other for funding and attention. Is that really the best we can do? Surely not. It became increasingly obvious to me that the entire debate needs to shift; and it cannot do so unless we figure out what it is we are reaching towards – the underpinning values that we want to live by and the vision of where we are going that makes our actions make sense.[3]

—o—o—o—

Hence: the infinite game. As I stated at the beginning of this introduction, the concept of the infinite game was coined by the philosopher James P. Carse. I first heard him speak briefly about the infinite game and finite games on *Ideas*, a CBC Radio podcast.[4] I then read his short book on the topic, written in 1986. I immediately knew that here was a metaphor with the power to ignite rich conversations about what it *really* means to live well together and how our current systems are failing us. I also loved its playfulness. If we approached life as an endless game with mini-games embedded within it, maybe it would liberate us to be braver, more imaginative, and more generous in our support for each other. First and foremost, we might trust that we are part of something, instead of attempting to boost ourselves with narcissistic fantasies about our individual power. (A case in point is the often-quoted claim, usually attributed to cultural anthropologist Margaret Mead, that a 'small group of thoughtful, committed citizens' is the only thing that will 'change the world'. This is not only wrong; it is a recipe for ego inflation, isolation, exhaustion and despair.)

Furthermore, the concept of finite games is an exquisite tool for understanding why and how life so often goes wrong. When we worship winning and hand leadership to the victors of cut-throat, competitive games, what do we expect to be valued in our chambers of power – compassion, wisdom, inclusion, beauty? Hardly. This, I have come to believe, is a key reason why it can be so *irrationally* difficult for leaders of organisations to implement deeply cooperative, democratic processes. It is not because these leaders are bad, but because they have been trained in a completely different type of game.

—◦—◦—◦—

So this book is for anyone who is concerned about how we, collectively, are going about life and is looking for alternatives. Carse's philosophy has informed this book as have the contributions of many other writers about social movements, environmentalism, culture, the human psyche, myth and religion. I have also designed an Infinite Game workshop, structured like a game, and run it with thousands of people. These workshops have produced numerous insights that have informed both my understanding and this book.[5]

In addition, I have drawn on my roots as a psychologist. My background in psychology has taught me to be cautious about making assumptions about people's motivations. It can be tempting, if you feel the world is a bit of a mess, to assume that the systems that currently cause hurt are motivated by hurtful intent. This is not necessarily, or even usually, the case. I try here to separate the system from the people involved, and tend to assume that most people, most of the time, consider they are acting 'for the good', even if 'good' does not appear to result. (That includes you and me.)

—o—o—o—

Part One of this book explores the implications of the infinite game and finite games from the perspective of society: How do our existing social structures appear through the lens of these games? What feelings and behaviours do our finite games engender in the individuals and social groups who enter them? How might society look if we attempted to keep the infinite game in play? I frequently refer to 'our world', 'our society', or 'our way of life', by which I really mean life in industrialised Western nations. This is the world these games are designed to describe. Two additional caveats apply in this regard: in the context of globalisation, much of what I say potentially applies beyond the West; and – in the way of generalisations – there are numerous exceptions to my claims even within the West.

Part Two is person-oriented: What does it mean to be an infinite player and how can we become better at holding the lessons of the infinite game in our lives? Being an infinite player – by which I mean sticking with the inner struggle to contribute to our collective present and future – is not easy. But if you are compelled to play, that is that really; there is no backing out and lying by the pool all day drinking margaritas. Maybe this book will help you, and those you share these ideas with, to muddle through a little better than before. Maybe it will even give you the sense of being part of something that amplifies what you do and makes up for your mistakes. More than anything, I hope it inspires you to get thinking and talking about the world we really want to live in, so we can usher, nudge, shove and *drag* it into being.

Part One

Society and the Infinite Game

Society is, in large part, a slow-forming magic trick. It is a trick that sweeps up aspects of human experience, adds liberal doses of bluster, and transforms it all into a story of ourselves that makes just enough sense to keep people playing along. Most of the time, the trick is performed so slowly, and with such finesse – the finesse of multiple players who work hard to keep the illusion alive – that we don't realise it is a trick. And so we find ourselves living within the rules society offers and even cajoling others to play along, being reminded whenever we waver (and reminding others when they waver) that *this is just the way it is*.

In the first part of this book I will attempt to crawl under this trick and flip it over – showing the messy underbelly of the finite games that turn so many of our actions into replications of the status quo. I will also argue for an infinite game alternative: one that digs into our nature as people, finds it full of unexpected treasures, and insists that these become the focus of our play – even when, *especially when*, almost everyone appears convinced that there is a battle to be fought and we must stick to our old, familiar guns.

The five chapters to follow are structured around the 15 pairs of statements given in the Introduction (see p. 8). Chapter One concerns the *overarching principles* of the game and covers pairs 1 to 3; Chapter Two is on *people* (pairs 4 to 8); Chapter Three is on *setting* (pairs 9 to 11); Chapter Four is on *knowledge* (pairs 12 and 13); and the final chapter is about *time* (pairs 14 and 15).

—o—o—o—

Chapter One

Overarching Principles

All games have a fundamental structure that allows players to identify the game at hand. At the most basic level, the infinite game is an opening towards life – towards ongoing play that encourages people and other life forms to flourish. We, as people, hold this game deep inside us. Its values are what we know really matters. Finite games, on the other hand, restrict, and in some cases shut down, life in their effort to limit the field of play. Finite games are essential to our quest to create the good society, but they carry the risk of obscuring infinite play and creating idols in its place.

1. Continuing the play versus winning

> The purpose of the infinite game is to continue the play;
> The purpose of a finite game is to win

In one of my early Infinite Game workshops, a man I greatly admire discussed afterwards how he could not get beyond the use of 'infinite' in the title of the game. It reminded him of his mother's religious beliefs and in particular her passivity in the face of illness and injustice. For his mother, 'the infinite' was a future space in which all the sorrows of life evaporated into a blissful afterlife. He felt its promise had encouraged her to exist with suffering instead of attempting to resist the suffering.

This passivity repulsed him. It represented, he felt, a fertile ground that fed human cruelty by its meek tolerance of all that is bad.

He had a point. If the infinite becomes a destination that numbs us to life then it is surely repugnant. Here, however, 'infinite' is an adjective. The adjectival form of infinite means: 'limitless or endless in space, extent, or size; impossible to measure or calculate'. When used in this way, then, 'infinite' is not some*thing*, but it is a qualifier that extends in all directions and across any dimension that we care to conjure up.

The infinite game most obviously extends infinitely in time. Although we sometimes talk as if we are facing the one time in history in which human life is truly in peril (usually due to climate change), this is simply not the case. I remember the bone-chilling, mind-numbing, life-supressing dread that accompanied my teenage years in the 1970s because there *was going to be* a nuclear war. My worried little mind was filled with images of mushroom clouds, burning flesh, and worst of all a seeping, invisible radiation that would end life on Earth (especially my own!). Indigenous people in New Zealand, Australia and other parts of the world have been subject to the threat of annihilation through the myriad of processes that make up colonisation for several hundred years. If you are not an indigenous person yourself, try to imagine what it would feel like to lose the ancestral land that is fundamental to your identity, familial relationships, and spirituality; or to be the one remaining speaker of your mother tongue. Further back in history (and still in some parts of the world today), there were massive famines, devastating epidemics, and chronic wars that put whole populations at extreme risk.

In other words, profound threat is nothing new to people. We have always been highly vulnerable to natural disasters and our own capacity to damage each other and the systems on which we collectively depend. But, closely accompanying this ever-present destruction, there has also always been an impulse amongst us towards the life-giving, the compassionate, and the forgiving. The nuclear threat, for example, spawned a peace movement that straddled national boundaries – the very boundaries the weapons were supposed to be defending. There is even evidence that Kennedy and Khrushchev, who were leaders of opposing sides in the Cold War, were simultaneously communicating in an attempt to avert the military conflict they seemed headed towards.[6] Here in New Zealand, a history of resistance and renaissance by Māori sits alongside the colonial story. This includes the establishment of a community based on non-violent principles at Parihaka pā in the province of Taranaki in the 1870s that became the home of hundreds of Māori families.

Disruption and rebirth, therefore, are an inevitable part of the human story. The issues of today may be unique, but the cycle is not. When we act for justice or peace or the natural environment, we enter a community of such actors: a long line of people who have gone before us, and will come after us. The infinite game never ends.

Once you understand that there is no end to the game, then it becomes obvious that to sacrifice the present for the sake of the future is a risky move. If we do this we become, as the philosopher Alan Watts has described, caught in a 'hoax' in which we are never actually alive, but always preparing for the next stage when we will finally be able to spread our wings.[7] On a personal level, school is preparation for work, work for retirement, and retirement for . . . death? Or, from the perspective of those of us trying to usher in social structures that promote human and ecological flourishing: if we can just get an ambitious international agreement on climate change / stop deep-sea oil drilling / prevent the latest free-trade agreement / get rid of the current government, then . . . what? Then we can relax and actually nourish what is around us? Even if our analysis is spot on and we do win the game of the day – with a hefty sum on retirement or a ban on deep-sea oil drilling – our life has still largely happened through the details. And if we have swept others along with us, so have *their* lives. All lives – actual, lived lives – count.

We have a right to seek beauty, creativity, good company and joy in the present. This may mean having children, spending time in nature, caring for pets, getting fit, learning art forms, working part-time or studying. We also have a right to be repelled by arguments that others' time will come: *The conditions of clothing workers in Bangladesh are not ideal, but labour-intensive factories are a necessary step towards the industrial development that brings prosperity. Their time will come.* Well, no, their time is now – just as is your time and my time. An infinite game perspective puts the onus on us to *live* and ensure others can too.

—◦—◦—◦—

By contrast, the purpose of finite games is to win. Winning is used broadly here to mean any sort of acquisition; be it the food needed to survive or the throne of the Seven Kingdoms.[8] It may even include amassing a fortune and setting up a philanthropic foundation that aims to (one day) improve the conditions of workers in countries like Bangladesh. These games are finite because they are about the pursuit of a single-minded aim over a fixed period of time. The play has boundaries: applying only to select people, circumstances, and places. And the game has rules that may include procedures, rituals, contracts or personal habits.

To be clear, we need finite games. They structure our collective lives and are a form of quality control. Bus and train schedules, training and ongoing development for medical professionals, building standards, anti-pollution laws, food distribution networks and school curriculums are all essential finite games in Western societies. What we don't need, however, is the plethora of *competitive* finite games that have become our default formula for getting the best out of people and sorting out who gets what and who is in charge. Competition that singles out and elevates 'winners' is our Achilles heel, our toxic magnet, our idol that all too often pulls our finite games out of shape; luring us, taunting us, confusing us, and silencing us into playing the way we are told, rather than keeping the infinite game in view. It is our version of the oppressive traditions or vengeful gods that other eras and cultures have developed to keep people under control. To really understand ourselves and to effectively reshape social institutions for the common good, we need to look hard at the winning-worshipping society we have become.

—◦—◦—◦—

Numerous authors and scholars have written about the tidal wave of competition that has flooded so much of the Western world.[9] As with any truly powerful idol, competition, and in particular the creation of winners and losers, is endemic and held in multiple sites – our psyches, our assumptions, our practices. We take it for granted that politics involves contests in which opponents mock each other with verbal venom; that our young people must compete for educational programmes and jobs; that universities proudly display their world rankings; that houses are sold to the highest bidder; that small retail outlets will fail due to the competitive advantage of big retail outlets; and that winning – even (especially?) if it means the accumulation of astronomical wealth – is an honourable pursuit. Our formula in brief: Competition = The Good Life. If you look up synonyms for 'competitive' on Microsoft Word, you will find the following options: modest, good, inexpensive, cheap, viable, reasonable, and economical.

So the assumption that competition is an appropriate way to distribute social goods ripples through us in myriad forms. Two core ideas, however, are particularly central to this assumption: the theory of evolution (as it is commonly understood) and the market economy.

–◦–◦–◦–

The theory of evolution – at least the prevalent Western version – tells us that individuals are destined to compete.[10] Competition is fundamental to 'natural selection' because those who win the race for survival and for mates will procreate more successfully and their genes will be passed on through the generations. Such a view is captured by slogans such as 'survival of the fittest', and 'the selfish gene', the title of one of Richard Dawkins' books. 'Survival of the fittest' turns altruism into a biological puzzle: surely it makes little sense for living beings to ever act in favour of another and against their personal interests? Indeed, when viewed through an evolutionary lens, even acts of apparent generosity are explained by the personal advantage gained by having a good reputation, or by the urge to protect kin who, as carriers of our genes, are the next best thing to our individual selves.[11]

Such an approach turns human history into a story of struggle in which certain groups are victorious over others either through warfare or through having superior social and technological structures. According to the Harvard historian Niall Ferguson, widespread competition is itself one such superior social structure – a 'killer app' that helped the West become the wealthiest of them all.[12]

In fact, current evolutionary theory shows that survival and successful reproduction involves cooperation between individuals and species as much as it involves competition between them. As the evolutionary theorist Martin Nowak wrote, 'creatures of every persuasion and level of complexity cooperate to live'.[13] According to Nowak, this includes bacteria that form strings in which some die to provide their neighbours with nitrogen, slime moulds that group together when food is scarce, and mole rats that eat each other's droppings. Some trees exchange nutrients and carbon with trees from another species through fungal networks.[14] In humans, cooperation exists within our bodies – inside which we have ten bacteria cells for every human cell, many of which are critical to good health – and within our social structures.[15] We regularly get together, figure out the best way forward from the options available, and create extraordinarily intricate systems of cooperation. Such systems allow us to exchange food and services, fly around the globe, and sometimes even oust destructive finite games and put something better in their place.

That we emphasise the times when life forms struggle against each other, rather than the (many more) times when life forms support each other, is not 'science', it is a distortion produced by our enchantment with competitive finite games.

–o–o–o–

Free-market economics is the second competitive game at the heart of contemporary Western societies. Laws and international networks protect competition as an intrinsic part of our economic structures.[16] Free-trade agreements are promoted with the notion that removing tariffs and other barriers to a supposedly 'level playing field' between nations will produce greater efficiency and, that magical elixir, increased material wealth for all.[17] The highly controversial Trans-Pacific Partnership (TPP) is an example. In late 2015, New Zealand signed the TPP agreement with eleven other Asian or Pacific Rim countries, including the USA. According to John Key, New Zealand's prime minister at the time, the removal of tariffs would earn the country 'at least \$2.7 billion a year by 2030 . . . that's more jobs, higher incomes and a better standard of living for New Zealanders'. The official position of the US government was that the TPP would increase 'Made in America exports' and 'support well-paying American jobs'; and Australia's Minister for Trade was quoted as saying it would be of 'enormous benefit to Australia', making 'Australia's mining-driven economy more competitive, create jobs and boost living standards'.[18] One might be excused for wondering how a more competitive structure turns *every* player into a winner, but there you go.

It may indeed be that the West has generated innovations associated with wealth due, in part, to sufficient social mobility and laws that allow new players and ideas a look-in – if this is what we mean by competition. In their book *Why Nations Fail: The Origins of Power, Prosperity, and Poverty*, Daron Acemoglu and James A. Robinson discuss the benefits of the relatively 'inclusive' economic institutions that tend to exist in Western nations.[19] They contrast these with the 'extractive' economic institutions that tend to exist (or have recently existed) elsewhere, three of their examples being Colombia, Egypt and North Korea. According to Acemoglu and Robinson, one feature of inclusive institutions is their openness to innovation that carries widespread social benefits. By contrast, extractive institutions serve to channel wealth towards existing elites.

It is almost certainly true that innovative phases of competition *between ideas* have kept Western societies progressing. However, as soon as attention shifts from the best ideas to the 'winners' who produced them, new elites form and genuine progress is likely to halt. This has undoubtedly happened in the West where, in many cases, large corporations are able to shape the playing field to their advantage. Examples include dominant food companies having access to prime locations within supermarkets; and fossil fuel distributors – in the form of petrol stations – having outlets on almost all major transport routes.[20] In both cases it becomes very difficult for alternatives, such as local food or electric vehicles, to get a foothold, because previous winners get to call the shots.

Competition between economic players also results in extraordinarily complex laws and contracts. This, as discussed by the economists Charles Hampden-Turner and Fons Trompenaars, is because competitive finite games discourage relationships between competitors who must instead rely on external guidelines and arbitrators as to what is allowed.[21] Think back to international cricket – there is no amicable chatting between players on opposing teams as to whether a particular move is legitimate. Each team uses the rules to their utmost advantage in an effort to win. If a player steps out of line, the umpire decides on the consequences. In the business world, this reliance on external guidelines means enormous amounts of energy go into studying, and playing to, the laws that define the rules of engagement.

However, just as survival of the fittest is not the sole – or even primary – force at play in the natural world, competition is not the sole – or even primary – force at play in the business world. Businesses are, in fact, highly cooperative in many respects. The concept of 'trust' has spawned a number of popular business books, and it is clear that high levels of trust allow businesses to put more of their resources and effort into what they are attempting to produce. If you do not trust your suppliers, you must channel resources into monitoring their product or finding new suppliers. If you do not trust your employees, you must watch them closely, which also detracts from productivity. Businesses, too, are comprised of people attempting to work well together, which means they figure out pretty quickly that this takes cooperation. At some level we all know, just through our experience of being people in a world of people, that niceness and compromise are absolutely critical to social life. Competition, we also know (and this will be picked up again in the next chapter), is of rather limited value.

–o–o–o–

It is an odd situation: we have become enchanted with competition, even while our experience tells us that people function much better when they are cooperating, rather than trying to outdo each other. To solve this puzzle, we need to understand what allows idols such as competition to take root. In part, idols take root due to the efforts of those players that are dominant authors of the cultural narrative. These players attempt to keep our collective attention focused on whatever preserves the narrative and the social structures which that narrative legitimates. Idols are useful in this endeavour as they emit a blinding light that makes it hard to look elsewhere.

However, idols cannot be completely fantastical; they must also tap an element of the human psyche. In the case of competition, the hook I suspect is our own, slightly secret and shameful, desire to win. We *feel* our ambition, greed, and selfishness. We have experienced the pleasure of seeing others do less well than ourselves. So, when we are told that these are natural impulses, this makes sense to us. It may even be something of a relief, if we feel these impulses strongly, to be told they are the lifeblood of social progress.

But we know something else too. We know the joy that comes from simply creating and giving and being part of something bigger than ourselves, without concern for 'what's in it for me'. This second impulse also feels to us like the more social one. But the dominant Western narrative says our analysis is not to be trusted. It is *selfishness*, not *generosity*, that helps us all. While this doesn't quite ring true, we remember our own selfish desires and we look around and see that the West appears to be doing better than the rest, and so the moment of resistance is lost. We have slid, not quite comfortably, but with little protest, into an Orwellian world of doublethink.

—◦—◦—◦—

To conclude, what we are surely trying to do, as people concerned for the common good, is to draw attention to the infinite game principle of keeping the game in play, for everyone, everywhere, right now and, as best we can manage, into the future. What we must guard against is believing, let alone replicating, the dogma that this is best achieved through competitive finite games. We must instead trust the instinct that tells us that communal wellbeing is enhanced by cooperation, and downplaying, rather than glorifying, winning. It *is* actually a little shameful to want to win. It is normal, yes (I definitely feel it – often), but the impulse to beat others is not terribly useful for producing the good life.

With this in mind, if you look closely at moments in which you sense the infinite game is in play and moments in which fierce competition is in play, I think you will find that they rarely coincide. Competition tends to turn us inward, away from everything that cannot be captured in the game's criteria for victory – including the basic pleasure of *being*. The infinite game turns us outward, towards the entire scope of human possibility. Of course, competition isn't all bad (more on this later). But it is certainly not all good. And if we rely on it as the key to human motivation, it distracts us from the work needed to bring people together and tackle the issues we face.

In Chapter Two, I will explore further the emotions of competition and the effect these have on our relations with each other. The next section, however, addresses how we can use ourselves as our own authority to determine what we most deeply value. These 'infinite' values can then be used to recalibrate our finite games so that they serve us, and not the other way around.

2. Infinite and finite values

> The infinite game is played with that which we value for its own
> sake; Finite games are played with the values relevant to the game

Until recently, we in the West could call on God as our authority on what was of ultimate value.[22] According to the religious scholar Karen Armstrong, God was initially articulated during the Axial Age that started around three thousand years ago in Europe and Asia.[23] He (or more appropriately 'it', but we will stick with 'He' for now) functioned as a stable point, a symbolic talisman if you like, that allowed people to reflect on what it means to flourish as individuals and as communities. God also represented the natural world – 'creation' – with its vastness, beauty and relentless power.

Importantly, the monotheistic religions that developed during the Axial Age assumed that people of faith directly experienced God. William James analysed autobiographical Christian texts in his 1902 book *The Varieties of Religious Experience: A Study in Human Nature*, and provides many vivid examples of conversions in which people 'sensed' the presence of God and were filled with '[a]n assurance of safety and a temper of peace, and, in relation to others, a preponderance of loving affections'.[24] Similar feelings are associated with God in Islam and Judaism.[25] 'The idea of divine love', Adjoa Florencia Jones de Almeida wrote in relation to liberation theology, '. . . can transform any situation, no matter how hopeless it may seem.'[26] When viewed in this way, God is a truly magnificent and deeply inspiring ideal – a means of articulating our most generous, hopeful selves; and of giving this side of our nature public legitimation.

God has not, however, stayed put as an inspiring symbol of use in our collective and individual search to live well. Instead, God has been misused in all the ways symbols tend to be when they are transformed into idols and used to consolidate power and maintain bureaucracies. We are only too familiar with religious conflicts such as the Christian Crusades, 'the Troubles' in Northern Ireland, and more recently Islamic terrorist sects. Then there are the more intimate strangleholds that religious doctrine can impose. Requiring 'belief' is one such stranglehold imposed by some forms of Christianity, as it demands that we suppress our rational minds in order to be part of the community. Restrictive clothing – such as full purdah for women – or forbidding contraception or homosexuality are others.

In modern Western society, God – as a generally accepted authority that represents what we know to be most precious and to breathe life into the world we live in – has vanished. This has certainly been my experience when meeting with environmental, community, government and educational groups throughout the Western world. God may be real to some individuals, but not as a way of people in these groups talking to each other.

This leaves a hole. If we cannot call on God, what is the basis for our sense of the good? How do we stake out common ground and say, 'Let us agree to use this source as the foundation of our play, the legitimate authority we keep returning to in order to make sure we are on the right track'? Well, I am not sure we have much choice but to turn to the force that conjured God into being in the first place – ourselves.[27] More specifically, we need to re-seek and legitimize that part of each of us that knows, simply because we are people growing up as people, what it means to flourish.

In the remainder of this section, then, I make the case for trusting that people know what it is to flourish and that this results in a pool of infinite values that ripples through human communities. It is these values that we need to turn and return to if we want to keep the infinite game in play.

—o—o—o—

To start, I am assuming that the good life and flourishing are synonymous. That is, the good life exists to the extent that people and other life forms are vibrant, healthy and full of life. I am also assuming that this means the life forms in question are doing what it is most in their nature to do. And *this* means that flourishing people are particularly people-like. These assumptions are perhaps best understood by imagining another type of animal, let's say a bird. A bird flourishes (that is, it is vibrant, healthy and full of life) when it is being bird-like. This may include flying, seeking a mate, building a nest, foraging for food, and so on. This is why, as Michael Pollan has argued in his book *The Omnivore's Dilemma*, putting chickens in tiny cages is cruel, because it prevents them from doing what chickens are inclined to do, such as moving around and socialising.[28] They are unable to be fully chicken-like and so they cannot be said to be flourishing. It also seems reasonable to assume that chickens 'feel right' in some sense when they are being chicken-like. Feeling right is the psychological feedback loop that helps to maintain these actions.

In the same way, then, being people-like involves doing what it is in our nature, as people, to do. Just like chickens, we have the impulse to move around and socialise. We are also inclined to use tools and make artworks, listen to and tell stories, enter sexual partnerships and have children whom we want to protect, explore our surroundings, and seek explanations for how life came to be and what happens when we die. These activities generally feel right to us and tend to induce what we recognise as positive emotions such as joy, interest, a sense of belonging, or existential comfort. It is also vital that we can direct our own engagement with these activities, as a sense of 'freedom' or 'authenticity' is at the core of being people-like and thus flourishing.[29] It is hard to imagine, for example, a young woman feeling right in this sense about an arranged marriage in which she is *required* to marry and have sex with a man she isn't attracted to. Or, in more recent times (at least in a Western context), a young woman feeling right about being expected to give up her baby for adoption if she is not married.

It is important not to get lost in the details here. Yes, you can argue that some arranged marriages result in affection between the couple concerned, or that some women do not feel a strong bond to their baby so adoption in difficult circumstances *does* feel right to them. I am not trying to claim that the exact details of flourishing can be precisely articulated and are identical for all people all the time. Individual variation is part of our nature too – and is one reason why authenticity is so important, as we cannot assume to know the peculiarities of another. Life choices are also excruciatingly hard at times – freedom does not remove the need to choose a path even when it is as clear as mud which is the right one; in fact, it puts the onus all on us. I am just claiming that, at a general level, flourishing involves being true to the tendencies of our species, that we are all seeking to flourish, and that we have feedback loops in the form of feelings or intuitions that signal if we are on the right track.

––◦–◦–◦––

It is a little more complex to claim, as I also am here, that we have a feeling for collective flourishing. To do so, we need an inbuilt mechanism that reaches beyond our individual lives. Fortunately, we have such a mechanism: empathy. (We also have other ways of feeling for the collective, should empathy fail us, as I will come to.) Empathy involves knowing how it feels to suffer, recognising when another is suffering, and having an emotional response to another's suffering. To use a simple example, I know what physical pain feels like, so when I am out walking with a group and see someone stub his toe I feel empathy, a wince of recognition for his pain. This is helped if I can see signs of pain in his face. Empathy almost certainly exists in all cultures and is part of our nature as people.[30] It is, if you like, an ability to generalise – to assume that if I feel, others feel; and to recognise the signs of those feelings in others. Furthermore, empathy entwines us. It means that your welfare has emotional consequences for me.

The Australian philosopher Clive Hamilton has presented a compelling case for this identification with the other as having an even deeper base than the one I have described. According to Hamilton, it lies in our intuitive ability to recognise the underlying oneness of life – what he calls the 'noumenon'. Versions of oneness indeed echo through much literature that attempts to position people as part of broader life systems. 'Inter-Be' is a lovely, gentle example from the Buddhist writings of Thich Nhat Hanh. The Norwegian philosopher Arne Naess wrote about the 'ecological self' as an identity that comes from 'broadening and deepening ourselves' and so being able to act 'beautifully' and with 'joy' towards others; rather than feeling duty-bound or morally obliged to do so.[31] While people most readily feel this connection or merging with other people, and especially the people we are closest to, this feeling can extend to the whole of existence.

Our desire to be accepted by others also contributes to our feeling for collective flourishing. We want *very much* to be liked and included in the group in which we find ourselves. In most circumstances, the easiest route to being accepted is through helping others, or at least not impeding their wellbeing. So our default position is to be helpful and warm – by giving directions to a stranger, welcoming a newcomer to our workplace, fixing a relative's computer, or looking after a neighbour's child. When we are helpful, we usually get an immediate reward. This may just be a smile and thanks, but as deeply social beings that is often enough to make us feel right and encourage us to act in that way again. Conversely, when we stand in another's way – by firing an employee, insisting our teenager stay home instead of going to a party the night before an exam, or telling a friend he can't sleep on your only couch indefinitely, their displeasure makes us feel uncomfortable. We may still know we did what we needed to, but it carries a psychological cost. Life feels better when we are getting along.

We even seem to readily formulate and internalise principles that promote cooperative living. One of the reasons why we may, albeit uncomfortably, fire an employee is that she is bullying another employee. However much we yearn to ignore the situation, we know that life is out of kilter and it is up to us to sort it out. Research by Larry Nucci, Elliot Turiel and their colleagues suggests that this feeling for the wellbeing of the collective develops in childhood. They conducted interviews with children in numerous countries including the USA, Brazil, China and Zambia, and found that two principles really matter to children: you should not harm someone who has not harmed you, and you should be fair.[32] Children will say, for example, that it is wrong to throw sand in the eyes of someone else for the fun of it, and if the class gets pizza it needs to be evenly shared around. Breaching these principles tends to evoke strong emotions: anger towards the violator, or shame or guilt if we are the ones at fault – more emotional arsenal that directs us towards concern for the collective good.

So, theoretically, we have a virtuous circle propelling human-on-human interactions. Through our feeling for flourishing, empathy for others, desire to fit in, and capacity to extract and care about the principles of cooperation, we are helping each other flourish *simply because that is what feels right to us*. And, in fact, that is how it works most of the time. Look around – small acts of kindness are the soft propellers of everyday life.

––o––o––o––

If our feeling for the flourishing of others has a slightly more complex basis than our feeling for our own flourishing, then our feeling for the flourishing of other life forms or the planet as a whole is more complex again. Notably, children don't seem to reliably apply the principles of avoiding harm and fairness discussed earlier outside the human sphere (although very young children may just assume animals have the same feelings as themselves and should be treated accordingly).[33] For example, children only sometimes 'feel for' a tree in the same way they 'feel for' another person. In research by the ecopsychologist Peter Kahn, one child living in the Amazon talked about harm to the jungle in this way:[34]

> 'It is like me having an arm or a leg cut . . . Nature is like a person, no, thousands of persons because it isn't just one thing . . . [A] person is like a tree . . . If you cut a branch off a tree it is like cutting a finger or the foot. To cut a tree down is like doing it to yourself. It is the same to our heart, it is not good. The jungle is like the heart of a person.'

But more commonly, children described harm to nature in relation to its effect on people. Here is a child from Portugal talking about why it is wrong to throw rubbish into the local river:

> '[The people by the river would be affected because of] the smell of the water, it should bother people to open their windows and feel that foul smell . . . [It would matter to me] because a person shouldn't have to smell dead fish or trash bags full of rotten stuff when she opens the window in the morning.'

We more readily see the consequences of harm to nature in human terms than in relation to nature itself because it is much harder for a person to empathise with, say, a tree than with another person. We recognise the signs of happiness or suffering in other people, as they are more or less the same as our own signs, but it is more difficult to recognise these signs in a tree. Empathy for a tree takes the imaginative leaps that the Amazonian child made. And failing to recognise what a tree is seeking or failing to help a tree flourish does not carry the same consequences as when we are insensitive to people in this way. People – unless silenced by the rules of a finite game – complain when badly treated. Trees do not. Nevertheless, at some level we do all 'know' that trees and the rest of nature matter. That could be due to an evolutionary history in which survival was facilitated by paying attention to the natural world and working with it, rather than against it. The writer Elizabeth Marshall Thomas saw this in her many years living close to the hunter-gatherer Ju/wa Bushmen in the Kalahari Desert.[35]

As Thomas describes it, the Ju/wa people in the 1950s were on an almost 'equal footing' with the other animals and lived without strain alongside fellow predators, especially the lions. As she notes, humans and lions liked the same prey, such as large antelopes, and had very similar hunting methods. They both stalked their prey, and the lion's short, fast run towards a target was equivalent to the human hunter's arrow. Nevertheless, they found ways to live alongside each other, such as actively hunting at different times of the day. Here she tells of an incident in which a group of hunters communicated with a group of lions that was after their kill.

In another instance, Bushman hunters had shot a wildebeest with a poisoned arrow and were tracking him, but when they finally caught up to him, he was so consumed by the poison that he was lying down. However, a large pride of about 30 lionesses and a black-maned lion had found him first. Although the wildebeest could still toss his horns, some of the lionesses were starting to close in on him, watched by the others, including the lion, who stayed in the background. Seeing all this, the Bushmen approached the nearest two lionesses cautiously, and very gently eased them away by speaking respectfully, saying 'Old Ones, this meat is ours,' and tossing lumps of dirt so that the lumps landed in front of the lionesses without hitting them. The two lionesses didn't seem happy about this, and one of them growled, but amazingly, both of them averted their eyes, and turning their faces sideways, they soon moved back into the bushes. Eventually they turned tail and bounded off. Soon, the other lions followed them, and the Bushmen killed and butchered the wildebeest.

Thomas also discusses how once the Ju/wa people obtained cattle, they no longer worked alongside the lions in the way just described but acquired dogs ('animal slaves', as she puts it) to keep the lions away. The lions also become unpredictable in regard to their reaction to people. The two species went from a stable relationship that involved an understanding between them, to an unstable one in which they were now dangerous to each other.

—◇—◇—

All this 'knowing', 'sensing', 'understanding' and 'awareness' I keep referring to is not primarily intellectual. It has an intuitive quality, as if it is both absolutely obvious and somehow elusive. For example, when we hear stories or see pictures of people with AIDS in Africa dying for want of medicine to which almost everyone in the West is entitled, most of us just know that is unfair. At the same time, we may not be able to explain, precisely, why it disturbs us. We may also see the situation as beyond our control, less urgent than issues such as climate change, or even an inevitable part of a cycle that controls human population growth. So we stumble and hesitate, and the initial knowing is obscured, until we are no longer sure it even exists.

Nevertheless, if we want to nourish people's awareness of what it is to flourish individually, collectively and as a planet, we must open spaces in which we draw out this awareness and show that it is shared.[36] This can then become the foundation for our play. Because we need to work with language, we will never achieve the perfect representation of what I am talking about here, but we can, and I think should, try our best. It is all part of identifying that which we value *for its own sake*, because we *just know* it is the stuff of life. When we articulate these values and realise that others hold similar values – because we are all people who want to be people-like – we have a basis for trust and hope that can, perhaps, fill the hole vacated by God.

—◇—◇—

For people to really feel they are part of a human community with shared values, it is not enough to outline scholarship that supports this conclusion, as I have just done. Ideally, people need to experience these values being expressed by others. Therefore, in the Infinite Game workshops, that is what we do. Participants are asked to name between one and three things of 'infinite value'. Things of infinite value are defined as: *Sacred, precious or special; of value for their own sake. They make the world truly alive. Things of infinite value can be in any dimension: an emotion, a relationship, part of the natural world, a quality or an object.* I often sense people's nervousness as this exercise begins. I don't give an example, and ask everyone to write down their infinite values. They then declare them to the group. Invariably, some people are worried that they have not understood properly and that they will sound silly or reveal something too personal.

I know everyone will be just fine, because variations on the same basic values come up again and again – *we are all people who want to be people-like.* And whenever a roomful of people declares what they know – on their own authority – to be of infinite value, it is as if a cloud has lifted. It really is a little bit magical – the realisation that after all that trepidation you *do* get it and *everyone else gets it too.*

On the next page is a word cloud constructed by Helen Madden, Jonathan Goodman, Rowan Brooks and me that shows the infinite values of 1085 participants in Infinite Game workshops.[37] To arrive at the words on the cloud, people's contributions were coded and clustered. Each word represents ten or more counts of a particular value. The bigger the word, the more people named the value concerned. The top seven categories these values fall into are: *human connections* which includes family, friendship, respect, inclusion, fairness, compassion, community and a sense of belonging; *human expression* which includes happiness, laughter and smiles, curiosity and learning, hope, passion, fun and artistic expression; *nature* including natural landscapes, wilderness, animals and planets, biodiversity and the beauty of nature; a category we simply called *connection,* which captures love (the most popular single value offered) and care that doesn't have a specific target; *personal qualities* including honesty, openness and self-acceptance;

vitality which includes children, life and beauty; and *spirituality and transcendence* which captures mentions of a life force, appreciation and wonder, and connection to the whole. (God, although mentioned, did not quite reach the ten counts necessary to be represented directly on the word cloud and so was included in the concept of 'life force'.) An eighth, smaller, category of *survival and security* also emerged.

So even without God, people seem to know the elements that make for individual and collective human flourishing – such as learning, artistic expression, laughter, hope, compassion, community, honesty, and self-acceptance. We also know the elements that make for ecological flourishing – such as natural landscapes, wilderness, and plants and animals.[38] This knowing is bound up with emotions and aesthetic appreciation. People said, for example, 'affinity with animals', 'joy in music', 'curiosity about the world', 'the click you see when you teach someone something', 'the smell of summer rain' and 'the warmth of sunshine'. In keeping with Naess's vision of the ecological self, people do seem to have expanded selves, and a corresponding 'feeling for' the collective good life informed by a call to beauty and joy.

Therefore, we *can* trust ourselves to provide the foundation for our infinite play (or we at least have a reasonable basis from which to act as if we trust ourselves, which is all a player needs). And this trust is brought into play when we sense that others are on the same page. Once the infinite word cloud was constructed, participants were shown it in future workshops – always after they had shared their own values. In some workshops, they were asked to write down their response on seeing it.[39] The four most common responses were: feeling part of a human community with shared values; feeling safe and reassured as if others could be trusted; the centrality of love; and being uplifted and filled with hope. As one person wrote: 'It makes me feel there are a lot of people out there like me. It gives me hope for the future.' Another told me later: 'Seeing that infinite word cloud made me want to write "love" on the palm of my hand every morning to remind myself of what we value.' (A few people were sceptical, suggesting that the word cloud would not apply to people in other cultures, people in poverty, or people at the heart of right-wing capitalism. I will discuss, and attempt to refute, the notion that the infinite game is a middle-class privilege in Chapter Two.)

The infinite game, then, is really an attempt to translate what is already inside us into a discussion about how to nurture life-enhancing social structures and personal practices. Its facets, which will be discussed in the chapters to follow, are simply elaborations of what people know it means to flourish.

—o—o—o—

Finite games are played with that which is of value to the game at hand. Finite values facilitate winning or the structure that enables winners to be identified. Just as finite games can be useful to the infinite game, finite values can be useful too. When finite values are useful, they lead to something of greater or infinite value, and so are of *instrumental* value. Paracetamol is, in this sense, of instrumental value because it will ease my headache and lead to a feeling of wellbeing. More dubious finite values are those that glorify the game itself or its winners. These are *extrinsic* values and are mediated by their social meaning.[40] A big house is of extrinsic value if it is desired because of its capacity to indicate success to others. Extrinsic values are brittle, a bit like a veneer. Have you ever watched a scene in a movie where a meticulously groomed woman, wearing perfect make-up, high heels and a designer dress, is standing in the hallway of her large and equally well-groomed house when she gets the news that her child has been killed? All of a sudden, her attire and surroundings look utterly absurd, as if she was just pretending to live until that moment. Extrinsic values then, are like the make-up that now runs down the woman's face or the antique vase that she smashes on the tiled floor in her grief: contingent and able to turn in a moment.

In Infinite Game workshops, after the infinite values exercise, participants are asked to name one to three things of finite value. Finite values are defined as those things that have worth *'because of what they signify or enable. They may be of value only to a particular group of people who deem them so. They can be in any dimension: an emotion, a relationship, part of the natural world, a quality or an object.'* In early workshops people often asked if these had to be things they personally valued, and so in later workshops I specified that they did not. People could offer things that appeared to meet this definition in the social world around them.

The word cloud on the next page represents the finite values offered by Infinite Game participants. These values fall into eight main categories. The most glaring category is *money*. (If love is a big bang from which the infinite game flows, money is a black hole into which many finite games collapse.) As Charles Eisenstein discusses in his book *Sacred Economics: Money, Gift, and Society in the Age of Transition*, we have created societies in which money can be exchanged for just about anything (it is of enormous instrumental value). Money can get us water, childcare, food, education, entertainment, time in nature, transportation, the airways, sex, and someone to listen to us. As Eisenstein writes: 'When money is exchangeable for any thing, then all people want the same thing: money.'[41] Due to the ubiquitous appeal of money – all of us want and indeed need it, it has had little trouble slipping its moorings and becoming much more than just useful. Money is now a marker of success (of extrinsic value). We want money, because to have money is to have made it in the eyes of society. To be swimming in money is to be a winner.

Status and success is another large category, incorporating social positions, appearance and qualifications; as is *ownership* which includes property, consumerism and possessions; and *domination* which includes power, war and competition. *Personal qualities* includes those that most of us would consider useful, such as ability, as well as more ambiguous qualities such as pride, ambition and self-gratification. *Systems, regulations and limitations* captures all the requirements of institutions including bureaucracy, authority, and politics; and *natural systems and resources* captures the way in which the natural world is used in service of human structures. This latter category includes fossil fuels and other 'natural resources' – which are in stark contrast to the natural landscapes and life forms offered as of infinite value.

Values related to *survival and security*, such as food and jobs, were offered in both the finite and infinite values exercise. Life is manifest in a tangible form, and for any sort of world to exist, individuals must strive to survive. Such striving is, in this sense, of infinite value and certainly fundamental to our nature as people. On the other hand, the act of taking in the world to grow oneself, most literally through breathing, eating and drinking, is the most basic of finite games. And we must be careful with growing ourselves. When this comes at the expense of others' growth or bloats us to the point that we are weighed down by what we have acquired, we have lost sight of what it means to live well.

—o—o—o—

To summarise: we need a foundation from which to build the good society. We used to turn to God as a symbol that captured the beauty of the world and the potential of human beings for deep cooperation and endless creativity. Now that God has faded from view, at least as a unifier of people concerned for the common good, we have little choice but to turn to ourselves. The good news is that we, as people, have a powerful feeling for what matters most. We sense the underpinnings of human flourishing, and somewhat more tenuously perhaps, the underpinnings of ecological flourishing too. These, then, are our primary or infinite values. They permeate the infinite game.

In simple terms, infinite values are what we are trying to keep in play and draw attention to when we advocate for the common good. We may each have one or two values that shine above the others – compassion or coral reefs or curiosity. But there is room for all.

Finite values may at times help move forward infinite values, but they are often a distraction from those values. Money is particularly seductive: *Just think what good you could do with a billion dollars!* But when we talk up money – or any other finite value – we lose touch with what we know, inside ourselves, enables life to flourish. We must also be very wary of reversing the whole playing board. A particular oddity of modern life is to imply that infinite values are useful because they help maintain finite values: *Save the coral reefs as it will bring in tourism dollars! Allow your workers to have a say as they will be more loyal and productive!*[42] No. The coral reefs and workers are valuable beyond measure. Tourism dollars, loyalty to a business, and productivity are not. A key part of keeping what matters most in play is to keep insisting it *is* what matters most.

—o—o—o—

But of course, we live in a world of money and status, productivity, competition and striving, a world of finite games. How do we recognise which finite games are connecting us with the infinite game and which are leading us into whirlpools of frenetic, soul-destroying activity that are doing no one much good?

3. The difference between finite games that are inside or outside the infinite game

> The infinite game includes finite games;
> Finite games may exist outside the infinite game

We play the infinite game every day. It has a thousand faces: when one person helps another get his shopping bags onto the bus, when a teenager spends hours practising backwards walkovers because she loves the feeling of trusting and extending her body, when a staff member sees injustice in his workplace and draws attention to the problem. In all these cases, it is as if the infinite game is close at hand,

and we step into it and play for a while. Everyone plays the infinite game at this level, as it is part of our nature as people.

But we also play finite games that enable us to give structure to the infinite game, at least for a certain group of players and at least for a while. We cannot just be spontaneous all the time: we need to organise ourselves. And this means creating finite games with their procedures, goals and agreements; games involving money, organisations and bureaucracy. Finite games that forward the infinite game will help take the latter into the spaces of the present and will not sabotage the future. In other words, they keep infinite values in play, via finite values.

Such games will rarely have perfect alignment with the principles of the infinite game, but they are the outcome of people trying their best. There is, for example, a bicycle shop near me that services bikes, sells second-hand bikes and employs budding young mechanics and people who have 'intellectual challenges'.[43] Every time I go there I feel uplifted by the somewhat chaotic space and the sense of community. I like the extra moments it might take for someone to check off what I want included in my service. It's like a glimpse into how shops might work if we did not, as is our habit as a society, pare them down to a slick exchange in which the well-programmed shop assistant seamlessly guides customers towards the goods that they are after (or the goods the shop assistant would like them to be after).

—o—o—o—

It is relatively easy to recognise finite games that have lost touch with the infinite game in the world at large. Every time I see a McDonald's, KFC, or another huge, ugly fast-food chain outlet rising up garishly on a local street, I think of all the idiosyncratic cafés they have prevented by their existence. I also think of the people-turned-robots inside, required to produce food and serve customers by working to an entirely pre-scripted role, speaking the words given to them and smiling on cue. Then there is the oil game, the mining game, the marketing game, the Uber game – perhaps even the whole capitalist endeavour.

The above are easy pickings. It is much harder to recognise when finite games located within an organisation founded to forward infinite values have gone off track. So it is worth looking closely at our third-sector organisations: those voluntary agencies, non-profits, non-government organisations (NGOs), activist groups, churches and so on whose purpose is to promote infinite values such as compassion, equity and the natural world. What struggles do they face in keeping their finite games aligned with the values they wish to promote?

The promise of this sector is that it embodies ideals that may be neglected by government or private enterprise. The most authentic way to embody these ideals would be to ensure that every layer of the organisation carries the infinite game spirit and that all employees and volunteers are devoted to the cause. This objective is captured in the following passage by Dave Foreman, a wildlife advocate:[44]

> Those who are lucky to have a job with a wilderness or wildlife club . . . must always bear in mind that the work of keeping wild things bears far more weight than one's career . . . It's good to have a healthy, well-run club, yes, but that is only so it is better at fighting for wild things. Never should we let our institutional/corporate needs stand above the welfare of wild things. We also need to keep our clubs from growing for the sake of growing.

As Foreman claims, the purpose of a wildlife club (or an organisation championing human rights, or a church youth group, or a charity for children in poverty) is to keep the welfare of wild things (or whatever ideal is in play) front and central. To do this, groups must be alert to finite games that may distract from their cause – or allied causes. This is hard work and it is tempting to instead make use of existing finite game templates such as 'career advancement', 'organisational growth' and 'corporate funding' and hope that the compromises are worth it.

This conundrum is powerfully captured in *The Revolution Will Not Be Funded: Beyond the Non-profit Industrial Complex*, a collection of essays edited by an activist collective from the USA called INCITE! Women of Color Against Violence.[45] The book outlines how radical values that challenge our current way of life are not likely to attract resources from the very system they are attempting to undermine. But, as the authors describe, it isn't easy to accept this difficult truth.[46] This is in part because citizens of Western societies are trained into, and are thus often mentally trapped within, corporate-style models with their hierarchies and restricted goals. Because that is what they know, they readily fall into corporate ways of organising themselves. The drive for funding exacerbates the problem, often requiring watered-down, less radical and imaginative goals than those that inspired the movement in the first place. Native American activists get offered jobs delivering social services to their communities and so turn away from their activism. Donations from private foundations shift black civil rights activists from advocates for system *change* to helping their fellow African Americans become *integrated into* the system.[47]

The spirit that permeates *The Revolution Will Not Be Funded* (don't you love the title?) is that radical transformation, which is essentially keeping the infinite game in play in its fullest sense, is a constant struggle with ready-made finite structures. I say struggle 'with' and not struggle 'against' because it is not as simple as just standing aside from the available finite games. Finite games are the games that enable us to reach and inspire people as much as they are the games that hold us captive.

—◦—◦—◦—

The fair-trade movement is another example of the tension that third-sector organisations face between playing within the finite rules on offer, and thus getting a foothold inside mainstream structures, and staying true to their original vision. In his book *Unfair Trade: The Shocking Truth Behind 'Ethical' Business*, Conor Woodman discusses how the Fairtrade Foundation, which owns the Fairtrade logo, successfully wooed corporate giants such as Cadbury, Nestlé and Sainsbury's, but by doing so may also have lowered the bar for what counts as 'fair' trade.[48] Woodman gives an example of one UK-based coffee business, Ethical Addictions, that by negotiating directly with a farming cooperative in Tanzania was able to pay US$4 per kilo for coffee beans, when the Fairtrade minimum price in the country was US$2.81 per kilo. To use the Fairtrade logo would have cost them 2.4 per cent of the price of the coffee, which they considered pointless as 'none of that would go to the farmer'.[49] Woodman also discusses how for the five years prior to his book's publication in 2011, the Fairtrade minimum prices for commodities were all well below the current *market* prices – and this is the period in which big corporates like Cadbury and Nestlé signed up.

What is the point here? It is *not* that Fairtrade is just another corrupt finite game. It is that it is extraordinarily difficult to balance the opportunities and costs of playing with the big boys, with the opportunities and costs of staying as close as possible to the raison d'être of a third-sector enterprise. The very concept that trade should be 'fair' and that farmers should be paid sufficient to earn a livelihood is a radical counterpoint to the dominant market rule that buyers should pay as little as possible – a rule consistent with the emphasis on winning that our society is often unable to see beyond. The Fairtrade logo, by becoming mainstream, injects that counterpoint into our food supply. This, it seems to me, is an infinite game move. At the same time, it may detract from more creative, nimble, connected plays like that of Ethical Addictions. As Woodman puts it, Fairtrade may make it appear as if almost everyone is the 'good guys'.[50]

Personally, I am ambivalent about many of the finite games played by the big NGOs. Just as I was editing this piece, I got a phone call from WWF, an organisation I admire and support with a monthly donation. After the usual effusive thanks for my support to date, the caller asked me how much I knew about WWF's work in New Zealand. She then proceeded to read a script about their work to protect the Maui's dolphin, a highly endangered marine mammal with around 55 adults remaining (a number I know well as I've done research related to the Maui's). She also talked about declining numbers of kiwi – when two days previously I had a meeting with the Kiwis for kiwi conservation trust who told me kiwi numbers are now picking up. But what was really discordant about the spiel was that she had an Australian accent! I told myself she could still be in New Zealand, but when I agreed to increase my monthly donation, she asked me – in her relief at having scored a win, I suspect – what the weather was like in New Zealand.

At that point, I felt like growling into the phone, 'If you are completely disconnected from the issues you have tried to entice me with then there is no way I am giving you more money!' Here I was being told to 'care' when I could not trust that the person telling me to do this 'cared' herself. I *did* care. But did she really care if I cared or was she just taking advantage of my caring? And did it matter if she was taking advantage of me when the money was going to a good cause? The encounter left me feeling both exploited and guilty for feeling exploited.

WWF are not alone in paying people who have varying degrees of prior engagement with the issues at stake to raise funds by using a standard spiel. Many of the big players operate like this. It brings in the money, and money buys advertising, office space and human time. But the finite game of fundraising in this way also tarnishes the infinite ethos. It mimics the encyclopaedia salespeople of old who knocked on your door and suggested that for the price of a packet of cigarettes per week, your children could have access to all the knowledge in the world. (I know this because, for 20 minutes when I was eighteen years old, I was one.) It risks leaving people feeling manipulated and suspecting that, if even the NGOs are using these tricks, then perhaps it really is a dog-eat-dog world.

—o—o—o—

How connected any finite game is to the infinite game is impossible to determine in an objective fashion. For one thing, in real life, almost all finite games are a mixed bag. For another, these games are slippery, depending on exactly how they are being played. But this does not absolve us from asking ourselves whether the finite games we create in order to forward infinite values – like protecting the Maui's dolphin – actually function in the way we intend.

Unfashionable as 'talkfests' have become, there is no way around frequent self-reflection if you genuinely want to forward infinite values. This is the only way to keep our finite games in good faith whether we are acting as individuals, organisations or nations. This examination does not need to be an exact, scientific process that adds layers of bureaucracy to what we do. It is a human process of observation, reflection and discussion.

If we neglect to examine *ourselves*, then we risk ending up with free-floating finite games that are simply serving *themselves*. We may even lose the language for challenging these games, and the capacity to recognise better games. Thomas Merton, the ever-wise Catholic monk who died in 1968, was a relentless critic of the church's tendency to protect itself rather than fight for the principles that Jesus symbolises. Here he talks about how 'milieu Catholicism' has fallen headfirst into the trap of denying its fundamental mission in favour of retaining its 'respectable and venerable image of itself':[51]

> Milieu Catholicism is Catholicism which is so completely committed to a social and cultural established milieu that when there arises a choice between the Gospel and the milieu, the choice is not even visible. The milieu wins every time, automatically. In such a situation there may perhaps be saints and even prophetic individuals. But the institution will strive in every way either to suppress them or to absorb them. Instead of exercising a prophetic and iconoclastic function in the world, instead of being a dynamic and eschatological sign, such monasticism is occupied entirely in constructing a respectable and venerable image of itself, and thus ensuring its own survival as a dignified and established institution.

Ironically, all organisations that spring from our craving for love, creativity, the natural world, justice, and so on, risk becoming rigid and self-aggrandising if they actually succeed. Success almost invariably means employing people, developing relationships with other large players, and losing flexibility. A brand (the Catholic Church, Fairtrade, WWF) is established, and it needs to be maintained. But we absolutely can, and I think must, still work to constantly assess the finite games we create within these organisations and keep adjusting them to refocus on what matters most.

—◦—◦—◦—

So, finite games are essential to human life. They allow us to live in community. But even when these games are begun in good faith they can become increasingly disconnected from infinite values. We cannot create perfect finite games that will work as intended forever. Rather, we must constantly adjust our games in light of what they function to create. This forces us to ask hard questions. Are the finite games around me (or us) functioning to forward the infinite game? To the extent that they are not, how could they be adjusted to better bring infinite values into play? Is it time for some finite games to leave the scene entirely and make way for others?

Chapter Two

People

There is a Māori proverb that is frequently cited in New Zealand. The proverb asks, 'He aha te mea nui o te ao?' and answers, 'He tāngata, he tāngata, he tāngata'. This translates as 'What is the most important thing in the world? People, people, people'. I don't take this to mean that other life forms are not also important. Rather, it means that collective life is *our* game, a game about how we interact with each other and how the practices that we invent interact with the natural world. In this chapter are five infinite/finite game distinctions that explore what these games mean in terms of our relationships with each other. In the fourth of these distinctions we come back to how, through the volatile and divisive emotions they generate, highly competitive finite games may function to separate us from each other.

4. Invitation versus selection

The infinite game invites others in;
Finite games include only select people

Sometimes in Infinite Game workshops people question whether the infinite game is a middle-class endeavour. They suggest that the values which underpin it are difficult to access or care about if you are struggling to survive. Beauty, birds, compassion and curiosity are good, yes, but security, food and a home are better. If you don't have the latter, then the former are essentially invisible. This query is supported by some psychological theories, most famously Abraham Maslow's hierarchy of needs, that assumes people have lower needs that must be met before higher ones are noticed.[52]

So is the infinite game really open to all? In theory, the answer is a clear yes. People do access the values of the game under the most trying of circumstances. Countless people have acted with bravery and far-reaching compassion while simultaneously dealing with poverty and other forms of oppression. Nelson Mandela's dedication to collective justice persisted through 27 years in prison on Robben Island and elsewhere. Psychological research has also suggested that people with lower socio-economic status may be more generous than those with higher socio-economic status. For example, a study by Paul Piff and his colleagues with North American participants found that, on average, poorer participants gave more money to a stranger, indicated that a greater proportion of one's income should go to charity, and were more helpful towards someone in distress than richer participants. This seemed to be due to poorer people's greater feelings of compassion and stronger commitment to egalitarian values.[53]

However, it is also true that being caught in the grip of a tedious, life-supressing survival game isn't conducive to infinite values. By definition, whenever a finite game dominates someone's orientation to life, he or she becomes focused on the finite game (largely) to the exclusion of other ways of being. This can be making a killing on the share market, or it can be wondering how you will scrape together enough resources to eat and participate in social life. If you must wait at one social agency after another to get food and medical attention for your family, you are unlikely to have the energy or inclination to volunteer at the Citizens Advice Bureau in your spare time. You are also unlikely to feel you have choice over the games you play – as long as you value your family, wait in line you must. But none of this rules out everyday compassion and the desire for self-expression and beauty. It also does not rule out the yearning to help create new, more life-affirming social structures.

Thus, some circumstances may make infinite values seem more distant, and this includes circumstances in which survival takes almost all a person's time and psychological energy. But this does not mean that infinite values are a middle-class construction – the product of idle minds oblivious to the brutal demands of life for the masses. As discussed earlier, the infinite game is about bringing vibrancy and life to all corners of the world. Is there any form of enduring human wisdom that is anti-life? That says beauty is indulgent and compassion stupid? Not in my forays into philosophy and theology.[54] If some circumstances crowd out these values, then an infinite game perspective would suggest it is these circumstances that are problematic, not the values themselves.

So one way in which the infinite game invites others in, is that it is based on universal principles consistent with personal wellbeing and consideration for others. No particular talent or skill is needed to play, and no one person can prevent another from entering. People can, however, make the game more visible by encouraging others to discover their talents and give generously of themselves. Peter Block, who has worked with many groups on creating participatory organisations and community building, puts this notion beautifully in a book called *Community: The Structure of Belonging*. As he says, our aim should be for people to feel as if they 'came to the right place and are affirmed for that choice'.[55]

Each finite game, on the other hand, is restricted to qualified players. Defining who is eligible to play is almost always necessary to organising ourselves through social roles and institutions. When qualifications aim to promote the greater good, it is still a move inside the infinite game. Ensuring teachers have adequate training and that mechanics know how engines work is obviously in everyone's interests. Even grading sports teams so that players of more or less equal skill play together can be an infinite game move.

Nevertheless, entry restrictions are sometimes enforced for the purpose of keeping particular people out of the game for no good reason. Racism, sexism, and heterosexism are clear cases of finite moves outside the infinite game. Sometimes these are blatantly applied, but increasingly today they take more subtle forms.[56] For example, it isn't that women are not able to be CEO of a large company, it is just that not many of them are. As of February 2017, there was one female CEO in the top 50 companies listed on the New Zealand stock exchange (up from zero for much of 2016).[57] I suspect part of the reason for this massive gender imbalance may be that women are less likely to want to play the CEO game than men, but it also suggests that most NZX 50 companies do not create an environment that welcomes women as leaders.

Infinite players need to be alert to impulses towards discrimination as they rise up inside themselves and when they see them coming from others. I once heard a woman who worked for the New Zealand Human Rights Commission discuss how she is careful not to always employ people who will 'fit in'. As she pointed out, choosing such people generally means populating an organisation with individuals who are as similar to us as possible. It also means rejecting those whose accents we struggle with or who may pose a challenge to the culture we have created. If you are the gatekeeper to an institution, particularly one with power and influence, then it is crucial you check your own biases and pause before seeking to fill it with me-clones.

Even more subtly, inviting others in does not mean just letting them play *our* game. It means listening to how they want to play, and, within reason, changing the game to suit them. This is a core principle underlining numerous critiques of how power is misused within modern societies and how to genuinely redistribute power, including Paulo Freire's pedagogy of the oppressed and David Graeber's writings on anarchism and the Occupy Wall Street movement.[58] Every institution that is serious about social inclusion should have a process for genuinely listening to and incorporating the perspectives of participants. There are plenty of such processes available, including group dialogue methods, deep democracy, consensus decision-making, and story-telling workshops.[59] It constantly amazes me that despite these rich resources for deep listening and threading people's voices into the decision-making process, so many institutions persist with dull forms of consultation that almost no one wants to be part of.

When people are excluded from games they would rather like to play, all that human possibility and energy has got to go somewhere. For a while, you can keep people in order, but after a time, life flows where it can. I often suggest to my students that if they are a member of the majority culture, and have never experienced being on the outer of an institution, try riding a bike in Auckland (where I live and work) for a week. Auckland, for those who don't know it, is a city of 1.5 million people with minimal infrastructure for cycling. The cycle lanes we do have are usually a green strip that is positioned between parked cars and the traffic, meaning you must be alert to car doors opening on one side and moving vehicles on the other. They often simply peter out in the approach to an intersection. This road environment tells us that cyclists are not welcome. Sure, you can give it a go if you want, but cars are the priority. Now, I am a classic case of oldest-child syndrome and I am generally extremely law-abiding. But on my bike, all that changes. I do what it takes to get where I want as safely and quickly as I can. From time to time, I ride on footpaths, ease my way through red lights, and occasionally I ride on the wrong side of the road. I am not truly welcome on our streets, so guess what – I find ways to make them work for me. If anyone dares question my tactics, I feel an almost uncontrollable fury. Excluded from the game, my energy turns into anger. If we want people to play nicely, then we must make it possible for them to play on an equal footing with others.

—◇—◇—◇—

Whether to, and how to, invite people into finite games is a tricky business. Because we must sometimes confine our games to those who are qualified to play (the teacher, the mechanic), we often fail to detect less worthy attempts to restrict entry. I invite you to closely observe the entry requirements for the games around you and consider if they are necessary and fair. They may make life easier for those who are in charge (which may even be you), but who do they exclude and what is happening to all that human energy? Do these games listen to players – especially new players who may not slip as easily into the well-worn grooves of the game? It isn't good enough to just hire a woman or someone of indigenous descent, the next step is to say, 'Your offering is precious and we will change our game to make it possible for you to have a voice in our community.' Not only does this step honour the player, but it serves the bigger game we are trying to keep in play. What is it to create a better world, if it does not challenge who gets to play the games that shape society and the way in which these games are played?

5. People versus allies, pawns, spectators or competitors

Infinite players relate to the humanity in each other; In finite games others are allies, pawns, spectators or competitors

Recall beach cricket. When someone joins the play, it is as if they step through an invisible skin that holds the game together and, in doing so, become one of us. Because they are one of us, we are willing to change the rules, at least a little, to ensure they can play. In a good game of beach cricket, everyone treats everyone else as a *subject*. That is, we assume that the people we are playing with have an inner world of feelings and thoughts and that their inner world matters. Infinite players relate to the humanity in each other. This is not especially hard for most of us most of the time; it is our default setting. After all, what is most interesting and fun about people is what they spontaneously produce by being themselves – their humour, gossip or physical skill. We tend to naturally draw this out of each other, if only to pass the time more pleasantly.

To play finite games, however, we can't simply respond to each other in the easy, intuitive style of people who have all the time in the world. Something is now at stake, and so you are either with us or against us. For finite players, there are four categories of person: competitors, spectators, allies and pawns.

Competitors are easy to recognise. We are trying to beat them. These are rival businesses who are also attempting to design the cell phone of the year, consultants tendering for the job you want, the woman with her eye on the same man as you, and the family whose house you are buying as cheaply as you can. While we cooperate with competitors insofar as both parties agree to follow the rules, the core relationship is one of emotional distance and formalised engagement.

Spectators watch and cheer when appropriate but they remain outside the core of the game. Think of Facebook friends who 'like' the commentary and photos about your holiday, the students at school prize-giving ceremonies who clap the awards given to their peers, or parents who stand on the sidelines of a soccer game encouraging their six-year-old to play hard. Spectators are valuable because they escalate the excitement of many games. It is hard, for example, to imagine the World Cup in soccer or rugby without the drama of the fans. What would be the point if no one, besides the players, cared who won?

Allies are those who are with us, and who are more or less our equals in the game. In a sports game, the players on the same team are allies in this sense. In wars, independent nations can also be allies. If someone or a group is our ally, then we must take some account of their feelings and thoughts because they have a choice about playing with us and we can't afford to take them for granted. Allies also contribute useful ideas and strategies that improve the chance we will achieve our goal. As I am sure you have encountered, one of life's exhilarating experiences is working with a well-functioning team to produce an outcome.

Pawns sometimes look like one of the other three roles, but they are not so much *playing* as they are *being played*. Pawns can be difficult to recognise and it is very hard to justify pawns in finite games that are designed to promote the infinite game. Therefore, we will go into some detail on pawns now.

---◦—◦—◦---

If you want to find a pawn, there are few better places to look than inside a war. As Bernie De Koven, a game designer and champion of play, wrote:[60]

> No one, as yet, has managed to play in what we call a modern war. There are some who feel as though they are playing, but there are others, at the other end of the missiles and bombs, who would, if they could, like to be left out of the game.

In this example, as De Koven points out, when we bomb people who have had no choice about entering the game of war, they cannot be said to be players. They are, instead, pawns. They are people used purely to serve the ends of other people, with no corresponding opportunity to also get something from the interaction. This is the very opposite of infinite play in which people respond to the humanity in each other. It is also different from more benign or helpful forms of finite play in which allies, competitors and spectators have an implicit or explicit contract setting out how they will treat each other, and where there are mechanisms in place to ensure that these contracts are more or less honoured.

But the civilians who are bombed in the course of war are not its only pawns. War tends to create other pawns too. First, once the leaders arrange for their nation to be at war, their own young men, and sometimes women, are used as pawns. Take, for example, Britain's entry to World War II. When, on 3 September 1939, Neville Chamberlain announced to the nation he governed that 'this country is at war with Germany', he also assumed that young British men would fight. While this assumption may not have been unreasonable, *their willingness to do so was moot*. To ensure this compliance, the National Service (Armed Forces) Act required all men between the ages of 18 and 41 to join the army if called upon to do so. By the end of the war, women too, could be conscripted. Potential conscripts could be excused – at least from combat – but only if they met particular criteria. (And if they were excused, they paid a price in terms of social standing, but that is another story.) Overall, then, the war functioned to suck young men into combat without giving them the opportunity to actively accept, let alone negotiate, their terms of entry. Even if some were allies by the definition we are using here – that is, willing players who wanted to help Britain win – many were undoubtedly pawns.

I deliberately picked World War II as the example here, because I have often heard it discussed as a 'just war' from the perspective of Britain and her comrades in arms. Only the day before I wrote this paragraph, someone in an Infinite Game workshop said, 'Not all war is bad – take World War II, we all know Hitler had to be stopped.' When pushed a little by me, he referred, as many people do, to the Jewish Holocaust, an event that has come to symbolise 'great evil'. To even wonder if Britain and her allies had alternatives to war is, by pseudo-logical extension, the equivalent of condoning 'great evil'. What this dogma does is ensure that the spectators to the war – in this case those of us who learn about it from our elders – are another type of pawn. We are not invited to take a position and cheer if we choose; we are simply allocated the role of being grateful to those who went before us for ensuring we are not living in a fascist world.

In 2014 I visited the Anne Frank House in Amsterdam with my daughter Carla, who was fourteen at the time – the same age as Anne Frank when she went into hiding. We waited in line for an hour and a half because it was July and we had not ordered our tickets in advance. As we walked through the house, I kept wondering what Anne, with the open-minded curiosity and vibrancy of a well-loved teenager, would have thought of the telling of the Jewish Holocaust and the formation of Israel. I wondered if she would have delighted in 'her people' gaining territory they could call their own and eagerly volunteered to defend it by military force. At least on that day, while reading extracts of her diary accompanied by a girl of Anne's age, it seemed terribly unlikely.

World War II – the war that many feel needed to be fought – killed between 50 and 70 million people, resulting in it being labelled the 'most deadly' war of all time. Of these, five and a half million were German soldiers. Approximately three million German civilians were killed. Millions of other civilians throughout Europe died, often as a result of disease and famine. This is also the war during which nuclear weapons were developed and used on the Japanese cities of Hiroshima and Nagasaki. For the sake of defeating 'great evil', those who we now claim had right on their side turned *millions* of people into pawns who were killed, or enticed or bullied into killing others.

—o—o—o—

Killing non-players in your game or coercing people into being killers is an extreme example of treating others as pawns. But there are many less extreme, but still highly questionable, examples of treating people as pawns in everyday life. One of the most obvious is when companies attempt to sell products using manipulative strategies, rather than by providing information about the qualities of the product. In his book *Freud on Madison Avenue: Motivational Research and Subliminal Advertising in America*, Lawrence Samuel tells how, beginning in the 1930s, companies used Freud's psychoanalytic techniques to investigate and then play on people's hidden desires and motivations (referred to below as 'ids'), to encourage them to buy, buy, buy:[61]

> [Freud's] concept of the unconscious, with its hidden desires that shaped people's behaviour, was a particularly powerful idea for marketers to embrace and exploit. Rationalization, the process by which conscious or unconscious acts were made to appear rational, was another psychiatric concept marketers could easily relate to. Projection, an unconscious mechanism people used to cast off their weakness onto others, would turn out to be an ideal motivation research technique, as would free association, which Freud used to extract unconscious feelings and thoughts. Freud was, in short, a godsend to Madison Avenue, his radical views just what the doctor ordered to advance consumer culture by allowing post-war Americans' ids to run free.

Modern advertising essentially bewitches us into the endless purchase and upgrade of material possessions on a gigantic scale. As the theologian William T. Cavanaugh has put it, we have been encouraged to develop an 'erotic attraction toward things, not persons'.[62]

All selling is a finite game. That is, if we have something to sell, we want others to buy our offering, and so our interaction is restricted in a way that purely open-ended infinite play is not. Our potential customers also become at least slightly pawn-like, as we are tempted to sell to them whether or not we sense it is in their best interests to buy from us. But it is possible to sell with the infinite game at your elbow. In this case, you are selling a product that you genuinely hope forwards human well-being, ecological flourishing and other infinite values. And it is offered in a straightforward manner that allows the potential purchaser to see its qualities and make a choice as to whether to buy it or not. A farmers' market is reasonably close to this model.[63] Usually the rule of the market is that the food is local and sold by the grower. It is on display and often available for taste.

In the world of the big brands, on the other hand, it is harder to detect selling that is infused with infinite values. Take Coca-Cola. The product itself is counter to current knowledge about human health, it involves the production of untold single-use plastic bottles, and it is marketed not for the qualities of the drink, but by association with happiness, friendship, optimism, youth and fun.[64] The entire enterprise manipulates our psychology for the purpose of selling to us as pawns in the game of growing Coca-Cola. What is particularly powerful about a brand like Coca-Cola is that it does hit some infinite values in its journey to domination, like a seabird skimming the surface of the ocean every so often to find nourishment. An icy-cold Coke *can* bring happiness and the company attempts to address equity-related causes and shows some environmental awareness. But, overall, the enterprise is aimed at growing itself, and genuine consideration of others in their full depth as persons is inevitably subsumed by this goal.

Size always makes it harder to stay close to the infinite game (so size is something we need to be wary of, as German economist Ernst Frederick Schumacher warned).[65] But even on a fairly large scale it is still possible to offer a product in such a way that potential buyers are closer to allies, people you invite to play with you, rather than pawns, those you are playing with for your own ends. A nice example is the package offered by Patagonia, an outdoor clothing and equipment company that suggests on its website: 'One of the most responsible things we can do as a company is to make high-quality stuff that lasts for years and can be repaired, so you don't have to buy more of it.' The company also offers advice on how to repair your clothes, encourages trade-ins, and sells second-hand items. All of this invites you to play *with* them, if you want to.[66]

–◦–◦–◦–

Pawns are the product of a scramble to succeed in the terms set by the finite game at stake, and of the inattention to the other this brings. I suggest you look at the games around you and see if everyone involved is a player or if some are pawns. It is relatively easy to identify pawns in the games you may already recoil from such as (in my case at least) the war game or the game of Coca-Cola. But look hard at the games you play or can influence. Are you offering your wares to other *people*, with the assumption that they have the right to decline them? Are your wares ideas, products or systems that you *really* feel will help forward that which we most deeply value? It is so easy to justify treating people as objects under the conditions in which we all operate. I feel this urge rising up in me when I am talking with prospective students on our university's open day. 'Come and study with us!' I want to say, when I really should be listening to each young person's story and then helping them decide if there is a match between their hopes and our courses.

Consider, too, whether you are a pawn in someone else's game. If so, is there room for resistance in your role? (It may be tempting to comfort yourself with the notion that you are powerless, but you may not be as powerless as you imagine.)

None of this means we must have deep, soul-searching conversations with every person we encounter. There is a place for competitors, spectators and allies – in other words, for people with whom we agree to a limited exchange based on predetermined rules. But surely part of our task is to attempt to ensure that these people know what they are getting into, and are there by choice. As infinite players, we need to always keep in mind that other people are just like us – they want to play, and not to be played.

6. Open-ended versus restricted expression

The infinite game values open-ended expression;
Finite games value expression only within the
mediums and rules set by the game

In the infinite game, the contribution of players is not fixed in advance. On the contrary, each person is invited to express themselves as they see fit, given an adequate feel for the game as a whole. In a large Infinite Game workshop in which people could only offer a single infinite value (and were thus bound by rigid finite rules!) someone offered 'freedom with responsibility'. This captures the essence of this principle well. Ideally, people would be able to act authentically – that is, respond to the situation as it appears to them – but they would also be attuned to the needs of others and the collective as a whole, so that their freedom would not create harm.

Cynics will suggest that a society can't run on romantic dreams of 'freedom with responsibility' as I have defined it here. They are likely to argue that authenticity and allied notions are an illusion (the postmodern critique) or that people need more rigid forms of control to prevent them taking personal advantage from the situation (the survival-of-the-fittest critique). However, authentic action is already woven into the brief of many of today's professionals and tradespeople. In my job, for example, I have various duties, including a requirement to teach at certain times and use the university's grading system when marking assignments. But I am also expected to use my judgement. I am not supposed to teach by the book or mark to a rubric that anyone could apply. Having *become* a university academic, I am supposed to assess the need in front of me and do what I think is right. If I feel the textbook oversimplifies a complex field, then I am supposed to add in the necessary complexity when I teach it. Not because I have been told to react in *this* particular way to *this* particular situation, but because I have 'freedom with responsibility'.

Similarly, as Robert Pirsig shows in *Zen and the Art of Motorcycle Maintenance*, being able to keep machines, such as motorcycles, in running order is a matter of responding to the machine in front of you. You must observe what the machine requires. Both a motorcycle mechanic and a university lecturer must be profoundly interested in their task to do it well. The boundaries between them and their work must be permeable, with their expertise informing their work and their work then informing themselves. Pirsig calls this 'Quality'. As he wrote:[67]

> The machine that appears to be 'out there' and the person who appears to be 'in here' are not two separate things. They grow toward Quality or fall away from Quality, together.

The best explanation I can give for why I *am* a university academic is that it allows me to express myself, to be authentic, to seek Quality. I am able, much of the time, to respond to the world as I see it rather than according to rules laid down by an authority. I remember when I did my first set of lectures being deeply disappointed by the mediocre student evaluations I received. But I also knew I could improve. It is as if there is always a hook in this job, something 'out there' that I can grab hold of to pull myself to the next level. And I *want* to do so.

People usually strive to respond as best they can to a task that needs doing, because to do so is to be person-like. But a society informed by the infinite game would take seriously people's desire and capacity to solve authentic problems. It would not always react, as our corporates and bureaucracies tend to, with more and more rigid procedures to deal with every conceivable scenario. It would, instead, attempt to educate people as to the conditions of the world as they were currently understood; and then trust them to respond appropriately. We need some rules, but these must *make sense* to those who work within them. No one, for example, protests because we must drive on a designated side of the road or because sterile needles must be used for taking blood samples. Yet plenty of teachers protest because they must tailor their teaching towards age-specific standardised tests that do not measure the real learning that comes from a public education system.

—o—o—o—

Valuing open-ended expression also requires a system that is not threatened by the weird, edgy and unconventional, but that relishes such qualities as part of the play. Angry, supposedly irrational people who insist that we've got it all wrong and have no constructive alternatives in mind are often canaries in the coal mine, suggesting where we have become stuck. They are, to use the language of games, necessary spoilsports.

Spoilsports are extremely annoying if you are enjoying a game. Johan Huizinga, who has written about the importance of play in the history of social institutions, describes them as breaking the illusion of the game itself. Spoilsports refuse to play along and act 'as if' the game is important. Instead they step outside the space in which we are, as Huizinga puts it, 'apart together', and show us that our little game is a mere trifle.[68] The more embedded we are in the game at hand, the more such players disorient us. If we are seriously thrown off course we may even attempt to snuff out their voices in order to prevent widespread mutiny. On the other hand, if we too feel the magic is fading and suspect that there is more fun to be had elsewhere, spoilsports are a delight. They are the people that name our truth, that stick it to the man, that take the risks we half-want to take.

Russell Brand, the actor, comedian and revolutionary, is one such spoilsport. In the past few years at the time of writing, he has persisted in jabbing holes in the status quo and allowing onlookers a glimpse into the finite games we currently live by. Like many others, my introduction to Brand was via the interview he did with Jeremy Paxman on the BBC in 2013.[69] In the interview Brand insisted that the current system isn't working. Politicians support big business rather than people's needs, the environment is being destroyed, and there are massive wealth inequities. Voting is a waste of time and we need a revolution. Brand's message in a nutshell: the whole game is patently ridiculous and we need to get rid of it. At the time, I was in Norway and had some evenings to fill. So I became temporarily Brand-obsessed, tracking down his interviews on the Internet. I found almost all of what he said riveting, and his energetic, seemingly uncensored manner refreshing. In all his talk, he challenged the institutions we hold dear, including the social script of the interview.

I think we've all seen journalists dish out judgements through their 'questions', while sitting safely back from counter-attack. Brand was not having any of that. Famously, in an interview on MSNBC he implied that the talk-show host, a woman, was displaying sexual urges through how she held the bottle of water in front of her.[70]

One of the academic listservs I belong to started a heated discussion on the appropriateness of Brand's approach. Some people on the listserv wanted to write him a letter thanking him for his interest in overthrowing the system but asking him to please refrain from sexism. To me that was all wrong. Brand does have a very public record of torrid sexual encounters, but he essentially comes across as *sexual* rather than *sexist*. When he challenged the MSNBC talk-show host, he used sexual innuendo and she was a woman. Is that sexism? I am not sure. In that moment, the power dynamic was such that it came across, to me at least, as an attempt to diffuse or undermine power, not an attempt to keep a woman in her place as a woman. Even more importantly, if you are in the lion's den and trying to speak your truth, it can be a confusing, disorienting process in which you make mistakes. Perhaps it is kinder to challenge power Gandhi-style, with gentlemanly decorum, than Brand-style, with ego and fallout and no overall plan. But kindness is not always the best play of the moment, and its opposite is not always cruelty. Sometimes, a touch of ridicule reminds us that it is all games, and even those with the shields of authority and money are just playing.

When I was younger the Australian feminist Germaine Greer seemed similarly attractive and important. I only agreed with about half of what she said but I was unspeakably pleased that she was out there saying it. (Now I think about it, she, like Brand, was well known for her sexuality. Perhaps there is a theme here: once you have breached major sexual norms, your life as a conventional player is over so you may as well say what you think?) I also love the students at my university who wear strange clothes. Some of you may remember the craze about a decade ago for wearing a petticoat on the outside of your dress. Imagine having the confidence to be one of the first to do that. Flash mobs, expressive graffiti, performance poetry, heart-felt displays to draw attention to social injustices or cruelty to animals, self-made tiny houses; when people let out what they have inside them in new and peculiar forms it is a sign that the infinite game is in play.

In my reading for this book I kept coming across references to 'poetry' and 'poets' as the one reliable counter-force to the conventional, or to use our language, the finite games that shape our societies.[71] While sometimes the authors literally meant people who write poems, more often these were code words for a deep form of expression that shows us the world through a slightly different lens. Poets in this broader sense pay a great deal of attention to how they are responding to what is happening around them. Their works are attempts to articulate this response. Poetry is powerful insofar as we respond to it emotionally with something resembling recognition: 'That is exactly how I feel/think/am treated.' Or sometimes: 'Yes, I can see what it is to be you, and you and me are kindred spirits.'

All the examples I've discussed so far in this section are poetry in this broader sense. When you are the first person to wear your petticoat on the outside or you challenge a complacent interviewer by shifting the spotlight onto her behaviour, you are a poet. You are also a poet if you give out pamphlets to your peers showing caged chickens with impassioned pleas to buy only free-range eggs. You may not be a great poet, because no one may pay attention or your insight may have been expressed more powerfully to your intended audience by others before you, but you are a poet nonetheless.

---o---o---o---

In the (relatively) free-flowing space of the infinite game, poetry springs up from individuals and groups and can offer great joy. In finite games, however, there is always restriction. Every finite game declares the mediums and rules that channel the action of players. This channelling is not always problematic, as order and restriction can be just what is needed. It is useful for everyone if vehicles are restricted by the rules of the traffic game, health-care workers by the rules of the hygiene game, and police by the rules of the appropriate force game. It would be useful, too, if we had more restrictions designed to protect that which we care most deeply about – such as laws that prevent us from burning all our fossil fuel reserves. Appropriate protective restrictions can free us to get on with life without having to pour all our energy into rearguard actions that attempt to protect what we value in a piecemeal, case-by-case fashion.

Even at the interpersonal level, rules can be liberating. All the deep dialogue methods mentioned earlier in this chapter – group dialogue, deep democracy, consensus decision-making and story-telling workshops – involve structure to ensure that every voice is heard and the subject at hand is the focus of the session. Having run several committees and chaired numerous meetings in my time, I am extremely aware of the need to formalise the dialogue from time to time. Every so often I get everyone to write down their response to a proposal, and then read out what they have written in order to avoid the anchoring effect that the first spoken statement can produce. I have also asked people to say what they *like* about an idea they disagree with. Sometimes people need to give anonymous input or a secret ballot is in order so that loyalty to one's friends or team, an enormously potent force in large meetings, is tempered in favour of a more reflective response to the matter at hand.

As an aside, I often say to people in Infinite Game workshops: 'If you are at a meeting and you are confused by what is going on, as if the entire discussion is missing the point in some way you can't quite identify, it is because everyone is playing a different finite game. One person is playing the *I need to agree with my manager so I can have my leave approved* game, another is playing the *There is no way I am going to agree with Person X because they disagreed with me last time* game, another is playing the *If we do this there won't be enough money to do what I think needs doing so I can't agree with it* game.' There are endless variations, but you probably get the idea. They are self-imposed rules that distract from open-minded discussion of whatever is officially on the table. Creative management of such meetings requires a new, collective game that can override some of these plays.

Careful, flexible rules can be useful for individuals too. Order, within reason, keeps us calm. And despite how refreshing it can be when people flaunt the rules, some rules can also promote creative expression. There is value in learning artistic or intellectual forms and building from those. Forms such as ballet, classical music, yoga, pottery, calculus and philosophy are the accumulation of centuries of humans tinkering with their bodies and exploring their minds and senses. Artistic and intellectual training is hard work that can immerse us in beauty and help us feel connected to the greater human community. Unless forced on us or turned into another way to win, such training helps bring out the best in people.

--o--o--o--

Identifying the finite games that promote life-giving expression versus those that shut down such expression isn't always easy. Games that are useful for some are deadly for others; and games can flip in an instant. However, as all savvy players know, you don't need to start at the margins where the differences are harder to detect, but with the most obvious cases. Which of the games in your world seem bent on pushing people into moulds? Which of these games nevertheless teach a valuable craft that nourishes the individual and offers something useful or beautiful to society? Which seem to have little function beyond maintaining the status quo and its current power structures? It may be that the latter games are already the focus of your frustration. If so, you are in good company, as challenging such games is a key part of what it means to push for change.

I also ask you to consider honouring spoilsports – not only the creative ones who make us laugh, but the grumpy ones with little finesse as well. They take it upon themselves to call out the finite games that are stifling our potential due to complacency, lack of imagination, fear, inappropriate use of power, and all the other forces that keep tedious finite games in play. It is tempting to leave those spoilsports unsupported at crucial moments, because to take the side of a spoilsport is to agree that the emperor has no clothes – which is almost always a risky play. But if we never take this risk, we reinforce the ever-present threat that to challenge power is to be alone, and thereby help stifle resistance and creativity.

An allied suggestion was offered by a participant in an Infinite Game workshop. It is that we push for finite games in all our institutions (including our volunteer and social-change organisations) that require us to stand back from ourselves and deliberately enter the open-ended possibility of the infinite game every so often. These games would say something like: 'Imagine that all of the rules are gone. What rules do we need to ensure that our deeper purpose and nourishing of each other and our planet is kept in play?'

The force towards conformity of expression is enormously strong in all societies – and not all bad. Its sheer strength means that it is extremely unlikely that pushing in the opposite direction, towards open-ended expression, will do more than slightly loosen the play. And it is when the play is loosened a little that new opportunities spring up – ways we could work together that are at least tiny improvements on what we have now. Besides which, who wants to live only as they are told? Surely, we, as infinite players, should create as much room as we can for people to respond to the world as they experience it – deeply, poetically, in search of Quality – simply because to do so is to be fully alive *right now*.

7. Connection versus guarded emotions

The infinite game may provide a deep sense of connection with others; In finite games victory may be joyful but must be guarded

When we enter a game as players, and not playthings, and respond by offering our best selves to the game, we also become open to the euphoria of deep connection with others. In the infinite game, there is nothing to bound or limit our sense of what we could call 'joyous expansion'. The underpinning feel of this state is the simultaneous appreciation of those we are with and openness towards anyone else who happens to come along.

When we are in the infinite game this feeling may appear as the grand euphoria of realising that all life is interconnected and so our individual self is of little import. This is the feeling I often have when walking in a public space on a sunny morning. It happens when I have got somewhere to go, but time to get there, and it feels as if everyone around me is playing their part in an intricate human dance that keeps life moving along. I feel no need to interact with anyone, but no need to protect myself from them either. If I am feeling philosophical, I may reflect on how everyone I see is alive *right now!* At *exactly the same time* in the long, long history of our planet! While the spell remains, that seems overwhelmingly more important than our differences. It is like tapping into a human force-field that enables us to connect to others without language or even conscious agreement to do so.

Some finite games can propel us into something akin to the interconnection with people and the living world that the infinite game evokes. This can happen when the rules of the game are so engrossing that we enter a state of 'flow'. The concept of flow was originally articulated by the psychologist Mihayli Csikszentmihalyi and his colleagues and involves complete absorption in an activity.[72] It can be experienced in any activity that is neither so easy for the individual it leads to boredom nor so hard it provokes anxiety. Climbing a rock face, riding a motorcycle at high speed, or solving a sudoku puzzle are settings in which some people feel flow.[73] When in this state, people are clear about what to do from one moment to the next, as the activity draws them forward.

People who are experiencing flow often describe identification with their social and physical environment.[74] This may even morph into an inability to distinguish their physical bodies or minds from the context they are in. So a guitarist *is* the guitar, the hip-hop dancer *is* the crew she is in time with, the teacher *is* his student. This comes from both authentic self-expression, and from total concentration on the task. Self-consciousness disappears. These moments often happen when we are engaged in a challenging, goal-oriented task. The game researcher Jane McGonigal refers to the 'unnecessary obstacles' offered by games – and here she means literal games such as golf or

Grand Theft Auto – that lead to players feeling 'fully alive, focused, and engaged in every moment'.[75] The obstacles of real-world finite games can have the same effect. Needing to overcome a series of problems in order to collect a hundred thousand signatures on a petition, or put together a twenty-first birthday party, provides something tangible to throw ourselves into. And throwing ourselves into a game can produce the exhilarating feeling that accompanies letting your *self* go.

—◦—◦—◦—

Letting your self go is impossible if you are in a highly competitive finite game and are focused on winning. The conscious desire to be first across the line means putting a premium on ourselves (or our team), which is the exact opposite of focusing outwards on what needs to be done. This does not, by the way, mean interconnection can't occur in a competitive context. But if it does so this is *despite* the competition and not *because* of it. That is, we sometimes forget we are competing by concentrating fully on the task at hand. Elite sportspeople seem able to do this. You cannot kick a ball between the posts in rugby in order to win; you can only do so in order to kick the ball between the posts. Similarly, when you are part of a team trying to win a contract or a quiz competition or whatever it is, you can feel at times as if you are all one entity, pulling in the same direction. Again, this happens because you are entangled in the task, and not focused on beating the other team.

When we are consciously engaged in competition, we are, by definition, aware of our separateness from the other competitors. Our purpose is to turn that separateness into a divide in which we have won and the other has lost. These emotions don't just damage the losers; they can damage the winners too. Victory in a finite game may be joyful, but that joy must be guarded because it almost always comes at a price. As I argued earlier, Western societies have become obsessed with competitive finite games as if they are the route to innovation, the best way to identify those who should lead us, and – the clincher – simply inevitable because we are fundamentally competitive beings. So, for the rest of this section, I will focus primarily on how winning and losing feel, and what these feelings do to our relationships with other people. I will finish by discussing whether a society that aspires to the infinite game needs any formal competition at all.

–◦–◦–◦–

The Infinite Game workshop involves a series of dart games.[76] After each making a paper dart (or aeroplane), participants are first instructed to keep the darts in play and include all players. During this game people throw the darts to each other, move around the space, and there is a lot of laughing and talking. When later asked to reflect on the game in small groups, participants use words like 'fun', 'everyone happy', 'created laughs and joy', 'playing for the sake of playing', 'relaxed', reciprocal', and 'full participation'.[77]

In game two, the rules require a single winner – the person with the most darts; and in game three the rules require a winning team of three people, who again hold the most darts. Players in game three begin with the darts they had at the end of game two. Games two and three generate a wide variety of behaviours including people who give up almost immediately, and those who play hard in an attempt to win. In the third game in particular the complexities of loyalty and betrayal come into play, and there is often intense negotiation over who will be allowed in a team that is vying for the top spot. When reflecting on these games, players have referred to 'divided loyalties', 'feelings of unfairness', 'moral forks in the road', 'passive, helpless, opted out', 'feelings of disconnection', 'boring for the people not playing', and 'only fun for the winners'.

Participants bring their own experience of competition to these dart games. Some enter with the assumption that competitive games are not for them. They feel they always lose, or they are unable to muster the energy to take them seriously. They may shy from the limelight that winning brings. Others almost instantly size up the situation and devise a plan to win. The challenge posed by the game is one they relish. They are inventive and flexible – if Plan A fails they devise Plan B. This is no even playing field, but an arena that is stacked according to what each person brings. If the workshop is with colleagues from a single organisation, there are added layers of complexity reflecting the pre-existing group dynamics.

There is, most definitely, a drama to the two competitive dart games, generated from the alertness of those who choose to play. That drama is fun to watch. The relaxed laughter of game one gives way to nervous, loud laughter. Sometimes this unites the room, like when a team who nearly won graciously bow to the room in defeat. But the emotions are volatile and flirt with danger. It is as if at any moment someone may take the game too seriously and the scene would flip from one of playfulness to one in which emotional sledgehammers slam into fragile egos and relationships.

—o—o—o—

Such emotional sledgehammers are the frequent companions of competition. But there are also rules as to if, and how, such emotions can be displayed. Thus, what comes into public view is rarely all that is happening inside the players. Most readers are probably familiar with victory scenes, especially those involving sportspeople, in which the winners look utterly delighted with their victory. They have succeeded, often after years of preparation. Research in the area of sports psychology has looked more deeply into what it feels like to win and lose, and, yes, the former generally feels better than the latter.[78] (I know you don't need a research study to tell you that.)

However, the emotional landscape of winning and losing is more complex than victory ceremonies imply. There are suggestions that losing can make a bigger emotional impact than winning – that is, the pain of a loss is often greater than the pleasure of a win. For example, one study of French tennis players found that if they lost to a player who was ranked below them, their perceived athletic competence declined more than it increased if they won against a player ranked more highly.[79] Another study of male Dutch rugby players found that overall ratings of positive and negative emotions remained stable before and after *winning* games. However, when the team *lost*, positive emotions decreased and negative emotions increased.[80] Sometimes, too, both losing *and* winning can feel bad. A study of the Japanese women's national hockey team found that losing badly – according to the authors they were 'totally overwhelmed by a superior team' (New Zealand!) – led to a strong sense of shame, but winning after not playing well against the Czech Republic produced almost as large a spike in shame.[81]

Ambivalence, then, is a frequent emotional consequence of competition. We'll look first at the ambivalence that can accompany victory, before coming back to the emotional consequences of loss.

One source of ambivalence with victory is that my joy as a winner comes at the expense of your disappointment as a loser. The closer I am to you, the harder it is to forget this. If you have children and live in a country that awards school prizes at the end of the year, you may have found that your children are only mildly pleased at winning, or even seemingly indifferent to it. When one of my children occasionally won 'best in class', I was overcome with the frantic joy of hearing my child's name read out, with thoughts like, 'Oh my god, [name of child] has been noticed, she/he is the best! Perhaps she/he does concentrate in class! I can walk out of here with pride!' When the ceremony was over, the child in question often threw the certificate at me in an offhand manner, responding to my pride with something along the lines of, 'Yeah, [name of teacher] likes me', or, 'It's only because they tested us on electricity which is easy, I suck at the rest of science'. At first glance this seems like a reversal of how it should be. My vicarious achievement should be less worthy of delight than my child's actual achievement.

But when you think it through, what would my child's social future at school be like if she/he whooped with joy at beating others? Pretty bleak, I would say. From the perspective of the losers it is bad enough to be shown up as not worthy of the special attention given to winners, but for the winner to then gloat would be intolerable. So sensible winners learn to play it cool, because every normal child is still far more interested in having friends than being the best at anything, *and so it should be*. They are too connected to the losers not to guard their joy.

Research on university academics has found that they, too, know to guard their joy when they score a win. Here is a comment made by a participant in a study by Charlotte Bloch of academics in health science, social science and the humanities:[82]

> 'One just doesn't do that (say that one has had an article accepted) and that's because there is always some competition going on between different persons in a department which means that one doesn't want to embarrass anyone. One doesn't want to, one doesn't want to (laughs a little), that sounds strange. But one doesn't want to seem boastful and if one comes and says – "I've just had an article accepted for *Nature* or *Science*" or another scholarly journal, one keeps quiet about it where others may find it easier to express I think. But it's got a lot to do with not boasting about it, one just doesn't do that.'

Other factors also interfere with the joy of winning. One is the knowledge that you did not deserve the win. This is perhaps what the Japanese hockey team felt like after beating the Czech Republic. They only won because they had the prior advantage of being a better team, not because they played well. I still remember winning the senior speech prize at school and knowing my speech was not the best. I don't even remember what my speech was about, whereas I do remember the speech that should have won – it was a witty discussion of whether New Zealand is the 'land of milk and honey'. Other sources of emotional ambivalence include knowing that your project proposal isn't as coherent as it appears, but winning the contract anyway; winning a music competition because the good people are away; or winning because you had insider knowledge or cheated in some other way.

Then there is the deflation of winning when you have lost this particular race so many times in the past that you feel as if you have just snuck through a wormhole in the universe rather than actually achieved anything. This is what it can feel like to get a research grant after six tries, or a job after 134 applications, or to finally sell your house after a year on the market and lowering the price every three months. The rhetoric tells us that persistence pays off, but sometimes winning through persistence can have a dull edge that does not feel quite right. This may be because the sense of mastery that can accompany some victories has a use-by date attached to it. If, by the time you win, you have long since achieved the skill level needed to win, the winning itself ceases to be a marker of anything psychologically significant. Even if you strike the odd win where none of the above applies – if winning sends you over the moon – you are likely to be subject to the pressure to win again. Now there is the additional pressure of having an identity at stake: a winner who might lose this time around. I sometimes feel that my own university carries a heavy burden by being 'the leading' New Zealand university. It tethers us, making it hard for us to play creatively. We know that we can win by the current rules, so why would we do something differently and risk losing our treasured spot?

So, winning, the supposedly good outcome of a competitive finite game, often fills us with emotional ambivalence. As suggested earlier, losing is likely to be an even more emotionally intense experience. I have had many experiences of losing in my life – far more than my experiences of winning. This is, of course, the reality for most of us as in most competitions there is one winner and several losers (although people will position themselves somewhat realistically, so don't necessarily feel as if they have lost just because they have not come first). I know exactly what it feels like to find it almost impossible to be civil to the winner when I thought I might be in their place, to be thrown into a frenzy of self-doubt about my competence, and to feel furious with whoever it was that allocated me the losing role. I also know the sense of helplessness that can accompany repeated defeats and how it leads to a refusal to play. (*I'll play any card or board game with you except Scrabble, Monopoly or Risk.*)

One of the most difficult aspects of losing is the expectation that you will hide any pain you feel. My daughter Carla did dance competitions for several years and when she appeared to me to dance well and was not placed well by the judge I not only felt angry, but I also knew I must not let my anger show. To do so would be to become one of 'those' mothers. It would violate the rule written on every competition entry form: that the judge's decision is final. One consequence of this rule is that any hurt or injustice you may feel in relation to the judge's decision is your responsibility. If you try to express your feelings you will be ignored or put firmly in your place. A good loser is one that keeps the cauldron of disappointment and its offspring buried deeply inside.

—◦—◦—◦—

Highly competitive finite games, then, produce different emotions for different players. And because I am feeling resentment, while you are feeling lucky, or I am feeling guilty pride while you are feeling the deflation of yet another loss, we all hold ourselves in. It is simply impossible, in my experience, for a winner and a loser of a game that means something to both of them to connect to the humanity in each other, at least until the feelings of the game have receded. De Koven, the game designer cited earlier, has captured the emotional barrier between winners and losers well:[83]

> Though we have been playing games together, the only effort in which we are usually united, the only accomplishment that we have all been able to validate, is winning. It is clear to me, now, that the result of such union is separation, always separation. It divides us into winners and losers, those who have achieved and those who have failed. The division then leads us into further division. It becomes difficult, now some of us have won and some of us have lost, to find a game that we are all willing to play well together. It was never our focus at all. Though what we have always cherished most is the game in which we are playing well together, winning takes precedence.

From an infinite game perspective, the difficult emotions and separation caused by competition is a problem in and of itself, because the infinite game cherishes every moment of play. It is not good enough to wipe such feelings aside with the claim that they produce an end that is more important than the means. What's more, it is actually very difficult to demonstrate that competition – especially intense competition, and especially when compared with cooperation – is a particularly effective way to produce positive outcomes. This is partly due to the way in which competitive emotions distract from the task at hand. Scientific rivalry, for example, often impedes progress. Ferric Fang and Arturo Casadevall, researchers based at medical schools in the USA, discuss several compelling illustrations of this problem in a 2015 review. The review gives numerous examples of how competition between scientists has led to errors.[84] Many of the errors, such as Kitasato Shibasaburō's dubious claim that he had discovered the bacteria responsible for bubonic plague ahead of Alexandre Yersin, appear to have been prompted by a desire to win. This desire led to shortcuts and guarding information, all of which slowed progress towards collective understanding of the phenomena concerned.

As Fang and Casadevall say: 'Competition probably works best when the goals are clearly defined and a field is technologically ready.'[85] This may be because a competitive finite game can help recruit players and encourage them to focus their attention on a specific problem, which is only useful for particular kinds of problems – those that fit within a predefined framework. They give the example of the Human Genome Project, in which the race to map human genes resulted in many teams working on this problem and a quicker outcome than expected.

Given, however, that money and resources – and just as importantly *hype* – were also made available with the launch of the Human Genome Project, it is difficult to tease out what, precisely, motivated the flurry of activity. Wikipedia, too, has generated enormous human effort, containing approximately 40 million articles at the time of writing, with no formal competitive inducement.[86] Perhaps the active ingredient for both these projects is (or was) the provision of a 'place to be' for people with certain talents. These projects say: 'Here is where you can make a contribution that will be noticed.'

–◦–◦–◦–

This brings us, then, to the question of whether a society informed by the infinite game needs any formal competition at all. Perhaps surprisingly, given my previous arguments, I think it does. As with the case of the Human Genome Project, competition can be one way to get people interested. I have been involved in dozens of competitions and awards connected to environmental issues, and they do motivate engagement. If you set some parameters and offer a minimal prize you will almost certainly get entries. The trouble is that the drop-off in interest once the winner is declared is often as steep as the increase in interest when the competition was announced.[87] So it is essential that in any competition everyone understands the outcome, feels it is fair, and has had their effort appreciated. It is also critical to avoid repeated competitions in which the same people always win. Very, very quickly, this leads to the non-winners losing interest, which is close to tragic when the project of living well together and caring for our natural environment is an inherently inclusive and cooperative endeavour.

Competitive tournaments are also extraordinarily entertaining, and so I suspect they will always be part of how we live. I love most board and card games. They are a way to be in company with others that can provide structure and tension to an occasion in which we would otherwise be floundering. Reality TV shows are often competitions for this reason – competition gives us something more than the cooking, the home renovating, or the sewing to draw us in.

All those dangerous emotions I have referred to come into play in these settings, but at least we know they are just games. The gloating winner of Monopoly may be temporarily disliked, but, thank goodness, she does not still own all the decent rental properties, the utility companies and the city's railway stations when the play is over. Greg van Avermaet, the Belgian winner of the 2016 Olympic cycling road race, is not now president of his nation. And the champions of *MasterChef* do not have the resources to put up restaurants on street corners throughout the world that sell only the dishes they have created. Tournaments that result in temporary victories at least allow life to keep flowing, rather than being held in the clutches of the winners.

Competition is an immensely powerful human force, fraught with emotions that are both exhilarating and dangerous. I am not sure we could, or should, resist it in every case. But I have no doubt that it is a less 'natural' state for most of us than cooperation. Competition is effortful, costly, and often results in a community that does not work together as well as before. It is best kept, then, within the confines of games we know to be games. Most of life – including making progress on meaningful problems like social inequality and climate change – is much better conducted in the spirit of the infinite game, in which there are no trophies to be won. One person makes a contribution and another person responds. Simple. This generous, spontaneous play is *what we do best*, and what makes us feel 'right' as people. Because it is so natural, it is also effortless, and thus efficient. A person who is working alongside others on a problem is not simultaneously pouring energy into guarding their emotions and their ideas.

—◇—◇—◇—

So what are the lessons here? First, I suggest we be extremely wary of using competition as a tool to generate engagement and ideas. There are numerous other ways to inspire energy and creativity. These include open-space conferences, setting hard problems, showcasing novel ideas and solutions, festivals, wikis, and giving people our time and attention. These may take more time and effort than a competition, but they are much more likely to leave everyone (or almost everyone) feeling positive about each other, the experience, and the underpinning cause. Connection is the real prize – it is the essence of most human joy and the engine of genuine progress. It is also how any social movement or challenge to the status quo gets traction.[88]

Second, we should be wary of promoting ourselves or our products in terms of the games we have won. I don't want to know if you are a world leader, I want to know the qualities of what you have to offer. Claims of victory might be alluring, but they keep alive a lazy, familiar heuristic: Winning = The Best. As long as we feed that notion we will stay trapped in a finite game mentality that separates us from each other and squanders our potential for cooperative progress.

The third implication is that, no matter how much we wish to work cooperatively, we *will* find ourselves up against each other in competitions for resources, time and power. We may be standing for different political parties, applying for the same funding, after the same job, or aware of 'compassion fatigue' and the pressure to win people's hearts – at the expense of an allied cause. To an extent, we need to accept this for what it is – the conditions under which we, at times, need to play if we want to participate in the social world. But we can simultaneously work to subvert these conditions. This may mean reaching out to other groups for unified campaigns, or just working behind the scenes to keep relationships as good as possible despite the envy, pity and mistrust that tends to result from competitive environments.

—○—○—○—

Think before you feed competition's fire. It is far from a benign tool that should be used whenever you want to grab people's attention. People are at their best when they work *with* each other, without the promise – and threat – that a winner will be declared.

8. Freedom versus obligation

Infinite players may come and go; Finite players
must be alert – to relax is dangerous

Freedom is the final person-related feature of the infinite game. It is a necessary twist to prevent the infinite game from turning into yet another obligation. If we are obliged to play, then we cannot truly play in the deepest sense. Play means willing engagement, and willing engagement is not possible if we have been coerced into the game as if we must play 'or else'. 'Or else' is a sign of a finite game that has drifted from the infinite space, requiring every player to be alert because to relax is to risk failure, and failure is unacceptable. Sometimes the 'or else' relates to our own wellbeing. *Take these vitamins or else you will die young.*

Sometimes, in the case of collective threats, the 'or else' relates to the survival of our entire species. *Dedicate yourself to climate change or else our species will be done.* You can feel the sense of threat in this passage from Chris Turner's otherwise uplifting book that showcases examples of sustainability-oriented projects throughout the world:[89]

> What else are you working on right now? What great project that would rest upon your soul like the many bars of ribbon on a war hero's chest? What that you would point to, and look your grandkids in the eye, and say, 'Now *that* was worth the fight'? I know how I'd answer this one: There's nothing else. Only this: To be part of the generation that beat climate change.

'*There's nothing else?*' I know what Turner is trying to say here, but there is *so* much else. Besides other 'urgent' issues – like the state of our rivers, the loss of habitat for wildlife, the conditions of factory workers, and the increasing concentration of wealth – there is also the essential, ongoing work of being kind, compassionate and fair in how we go about life.

There are untold other variations too – get this contract or else you will be demoted, pay this exorbitant rent or else you will be homeless, get your teeth whitened or else you will be a social pariah, win this game of cricket or else you will let your country down. In each case the speaker is using the appeals he or she has at hand in an attempt to get others to join his or her game. The others have become pawns.

When 'or else' comes into play, it actually signals the powerlessness of the speaker. You fear that what you hope for isn't convincing enough, and so you attempt to disguise it or make it more than it is – to dress it up with extra ribbons that might do the trick. Any parent reading this probably knows the feeling of powerlessness that results from attempting to cajole, bribe or threaten your child into a hoped-for behaviour: '*You're a big girl now, isn't it time you stopped screaming when I drop you at daycare?*' '*If you don't eat your dinner you won't get any pudding.*' '*If you pass this exam I'll give you $100 to spend on alcohol.*' Even if, by some miracle, the target child does stop screaming or start eating or studying, you know you have not really won. More precisely, you have won, but winning isn't the point. You have played the 'or else' game, taking the focus off your real concern (your child's unhappiness when you leave, refusal to eat healthy food, or apparent disregard for educational attainment) and shifting it elsewhere. Any compliance is not that of a player who is truly with you. Your power is flimsy and exhausting to exercise.

When we are playing within the infinite game, other people's behaviour is not our concern. We make a move and they – well, they may respond as we hope, or they may do precisely what we most feared. I am not advocating a laissez-faire approach to parenting or social change here. It is more about cultivating ownership of your own moves and accepting that other people will make theirs. Take the dinner example – one I am very familiar with as I had huge battles over food with my oldest daughter – it really does work (most of the time) to offer food you feel is reasonably healthy and your child will find appetising, and leave it at that.[90] No pleading. When you accept that your child's decisions are her own, something shifts. She may or may not eat well, but she has the opportunity to make that choice. You are not both on edge, hurling verbal missiles at each other: *'You liked it last time.' 'Yes, but this time it tastes disgusting.' 'Just one more bite.' 'Yuck, I can't eat that bit, it has something gross in it.' 'Everyone else will be enjoying their ice cream soon.' 'I want to throw up.'*

The parent who accepts she can't control her child, but is entitled – as are all people – to hold by what she values is working in the same spirt as many non-violent civil actions. When Rosa Parks refused to give up her bus seat for a white passenger she did not (and could not) force others to respond in a particular manner; her act simply said – this is what I or we must do, it is up to you what happens next. When Julia Butterfly Hill lived in a redwood tree for 738 days in the hope this would prevent the tree from being felled, she was making the same move. So are those who refuse to go to war or who boycott companies they consider unethical.

I have already discussed how the infinite game welcomes all players. The flip side of this is that the infinite game also allows players to leave. If any one of us steps outside the infinite space – abandoning love, curiosity, animals, beauty, and so on – then the gap we leave will simply be filled by other players. This isn't to say there will ever be enough infinite players to make the world as wonderful as it could be; there may not even be enough to ensure we don't destroy ourselves with the finite games we are immersed in. This is, perhaps, what Turner fears – as do many of us – that despite there being blatantly obvious risks to what we value right in front of us, we will be unable to take effective collective action. Even more deeply, however, I think we fear our *individual* failure to respond as needed. Cajoling others can be a means of deflecting from our secret knowledge, that I, personally, cannot quite give myself to the cause as I should. That knowledge is part of what it means to be aware that there is a truckload of problems in the world. *I really should be solving them in every spare moment, but you know what, I want to live as well.* I suspect that most of us only rarely hit that Rosa Parks moment when a clear action emerges that is ours to take.

—◇—◇—◇—

Another outcome of insisting that others play because the game *needs* them is that the truth is simplified, the message is exaggerated, and little depth of feeling is needed to participate. As with some of the fundraising tactics of NGOs discussed earlier, we may win the battle of the moment but risk losing sight of the ethos that inspired our actions in the first place. Our actions start to merge with those of less noble calls to duty, when the powers that be are asking people to act against their best interests, take great risks, or engage in ethically dubious behaviour. *Hey, how about you fight a war for us – a war against terrorism, a war for democracy, a war to restore the dignity of our people, a war to resolve historical injustices, a war against capitalist oppression, a war to end all wars?* If we trust that people most deeply value that which keeps the infinite game in play – and the evidence suggests this is the case – then progress lies in encouraging people to express those values. That is delicate work, and set back almost as easily when world-savers ask people to act out of duty as when the military-industrial complex does so.

—◇—◇—◇—

So when we are fully in an infinite game space, we are as light as a feather and as grounded as a tree in an old-growth forest. We know both that our acts will be blown away with the next puff of wind and that they draw from a strength that is deep and true. If we are alert with fear, terrified of dropping the ball, and dashing around trying to convince others to play with us, then we are playing another game altogether. We are playing the game that we probably loathe when it comes from groups we distrust – the game of manipulating people into setting aside their feeling for life (and the lives of others) for the sake of The Right Way. Instead we need to allow people to make their own choices while we stay as focused, consistent and values-driven as possible.

Chapter Three

Setting

The infinite game, our game as people, is played within a much grander setting – that of the planet we inhabit. It is not only in awe of life in all its forms, but it mimics the way in which life rises and falls within natural systems. As will be discussed in this chapter, the infinite game is a network, with immense diversity. It thrives on interdependence. We must be careful of finite games that attempt to take over the play, crowding out the possibility of variety, flexibility and new growth.

9. A network versus discrete entities

The infinite game is an open network in which every-
thing is interconnected, Finite games are discrete
entities that may expand or replicate

The infinite game is the mighty game from which finite games arise and into which they eventually disappear. We can work to ensure our finite games stay connected to the values of the infinite game, or we can work to build up our finite games as independent edifices that we hope will resist collapse. The first is the *network* approach of infinite players, who understand that to create the conditions for deep and full living, our games must be connected to the games of others and have porous membranes. The latter is the *discrete entities* approach of finite players.

Networks are the central feature of several current theories on how biological life works. From an evolutionary perspective, life is often portrayed as developing in a network-like process, in which all life forms are changing in response to each other and the material world. For example, Jessica Yeates and Niles Lehman, chemists from Portland State University, have proposed that 'a network of co-operating molecules could have kick-started life'.[91] Carbon, the core element of life, is probably in that core position because of its exceptional ability to bond with other elements.

Complexity theory extends the concept of networks to all complex systems, which includes the current ecological systems on Earth and every form of social activity.[92] From the perspective of complex systems, the parts of a system interact to produce something greater than the sum of these parts and cannot be fully understood without reference to the wider context. Systems are 'emergent' rather than constructed or fixed, as everything is in constant motion.[93]

One interesting feature of complex systems is that while everything is interconnected, there are still systems within systems, which we will call units. For example, a human being is a system of organs and blood vessels, nerves and sensations, and thoughts and feelings that act as a unit. While each of us is connected to other human beings and life forms, we also have an identity of our own. And we strive, automatically, to maintain our identity. Nassim Nicholas Taleb has argued in his book *Antifragile: Things that Gain from Disorder* that some units, be they people, organisations, nations or institutions, are more fragile than others.[94] Fragile units cannot respond to shocks and are vulnerable to complete and sudden breakage. A glass is fragile in this sense, as no shock is good for it, and some shocks, like being dropped on a tiled floor, are fatal. A person is less fragile than a glass because many shocks help people grow. Pounding the pavements shocks our bodies but strengthens our bones. Being told we are boring by a friend hurts our feelings but is an opportunity to become a more interesting companion. Our need for interactions with, and feedback from, the outside world in order to thrive makes us relatively antifragile.

To translate this into the language of our two types of games, this suggests that finite games which respond to the infinite network are antifragile whereas those that do not are fragile. That is, if a game is embedded within infinite values, it will be responsive to life outside the game; whereas if a game is focused on maintaining its rules and players are concerned with winning by those rules, it will be unresponsive to life outside the game. The former game is, in turn, less vulnerable to shocks and sudden collapse than the latter. It isn't quite as simple as that, because even relatively antifragile units in complex systems are not completely invulnerable, and nor, from an infinite game perspective, would we want them to be. At some point, the unit, be it a game or a person or whatever, has done its dash and continual adaptation ceases to be possible or desirable. Think here of the 90-year-old who feels worn out by life, the sudden boredom children feel with the possibilities that marbles offer, or a school assessment system that has become cumbersome and out of date. It is the bigger network we are ultimately interested in if we are playing an infinite game.

Fragile finite games (i.e. those that are relatively disconnected from the infinite game) can often look, and for a time be, extremely robust. They can draw considerable energy from the network, grow bigger and bigger, and admirers of them can replicate these units in other parts of the system. As long as players can convince others to keep these games intact, and this is physically possible, then society can convince itself that this strategy 'works' (often a clue that we are in trouble!). An obvious recent example of this phenomenon is the USA's Emergency Economic Stabilization Act of 2008, which authorised the expenditure of $700 billion of public money to ensure the banking system did not collapse when it was on the brink of doing so. The banks concerned were considered 'too big to fail'. And because the US economy 'recovered' from the crisis of 2008, it can appear as if the current banking system really is the best we can do.

Inevitably, however, attempting to protect any entity from the system around it is a terribly risky business and leads to all sorts of distortions in the flow of life. The protection of 'the economy' in most of the world's nations over and above clear signals of harm being caused to people and ecosystems could well be leading us towards a system collapse.

A case in point: in the New Zealand government's discussion document put out in preparation for the 2015 climate conference in Paris, it was estimated that a 40 per cent emissions reduction target would lead to a fall in the annual spending capacity of the average household of $1,800 by 2027.[95] To put this in perspective, the average household spends $73,000 according to the same document. So that represents a potential fall of 2.4 per cent in average spending capacity, which is about one quarter of what New Zealanders spend on 'entertainment and culture'.[96] (Of course, the loss of $34 a week would not even be noticed by many households, and one wonders why the figures were presented in this way – as if it is somehow 'fair' for any costs to be borne by, and evenly distributed amongst, households. But that isn't the point here.)

The eventual target announced by the government in July 2015 was a 30 per cent reduction by 2030.[97] Given the projections of climate scientists on the probable impact to the Earth's systems of anything other than radical and immediate emissions reductions, it seems extraordinary that we would *even consider* protecting 'household spending' over and above responding appropriately to that information. It is analogous to hearing that your child has a better than even chance of getting a disease that will severely reduce her quality of life by the time she is 30, and choosing to boost her retirement savings rather than take precautionary action. In no normal sense is it rational behaviour to choose the former path.

But this is what happens when we forget that our finite games are (at best) strategies for living well together *in our current circumstances* and start to think they are essential to the human project. We re-create them in new environments and hold on to them in old environments, in what seems like a race to stamp the world with just one version of whatever institutional practice is at stake. Massive Open Online Courses (MOOCs) are an educational example of this mentality. Their vision is that people in all parts of the world can learn from the brightest and the best at the elite universities (usually in the USA) who have the resources and reputation to reach well beyond their usual confines. Is this seriously what we want? To have the whole world trained Harvard-style? Similarly, notions like 'best practice' and 'scalability' are finite plays whose value must be very carefully scrutinised before they are implemented. Personally, I would far rather my children (and yours) were educated by local teachers in a somewhat inefficient and idiosyncratic style – errors, inconsistencies, prejudices and all – than by an online programme that delivers them the 'best' education to be had.

From a network perspective, practices are improved and players are inspired to give of their best through discussions with other players. In the case of education, the alternative to standardised everything is not a free-for-all in which teachers are unaccountable for their actions. The alternative is regularly exposing teachers to new ideas and giving them the time to engage with these and change their practices in light of them. Teachers must be part of well-functioning, peer-based networks in order to stay alive to their work. And those peer-based networks must, in turn, be integrated with the larger community. Sure, it takes time and energy to maintain networks, but it also takes time and energy to maintain standardised entities that pull against the better judgement of those implementing them.

—o—o—o—

It would change the world if those working in our core institutions – such as education, health, environmental agencies and politics – were able to respond to the information coming to them from the real world, rather than having to filter everything through the assumption that the entities we are used to (a.k.a. business as usual) must be preserved. This is, I think, a core aspect of what many of us seek as people concerned for the common good. It is a plea for those who are currently in the business of preserving and growing *discrete entities* to instead focus on preserving and growing *networks* in which what we most care about can thrive.

It is most unlikely, however, that those who are head down making their corporation or university or stock exchange or standardised testing method the gold standard are going to be advocates for network thinking. Instead, it is those of us who are not caught in the race to preserve and grow a brand that can, if we wish, use networks to infiltrate and disrupt business as usual. According to Edwin Olson and Glenda Eoyang, who have applied complex systems theory to organisation change, such networks can become 'shadow systems'.[98]

Essentially, Olson and Eoyang's argument is that systems are maintained and threatened by 'attractors'.[99] *Stable attractors* keep a system in place. For example, household spending is a stable attractor in maintaining New Zealand's economic system; it is something that the system as a whole works to preserve. Our standardised school testing system is another example within education. *Unstable attractors*, on the other hand, disrupt the system. So, awareness of climate change is an unstable economic attractor that, by demanding attention, draws some activity away from the current stable attractors. Unstable attractors can simply throw a little chaos into the mix. However, if they gain momentum, they may become *strange attractors*. Strange attractors are alternative patterns that can, and sometimes do, replace the status quo. For example, in the 1970s, when Finland implemented a new school system based on the principle that all children should receive a quality, general education provided by the state, this was a strange attractor that disrupted the assumption that educational opportunity should be based on individual talent.[100] This once strange attractor has now become a stable attractor in Finland, to the point that considerable efforts are put into ensuring that all children thrive at all the key aspects of schooling.

Shadow systems are attempts to create strange attractors. According to Olson and Eoyang, shadow systems are alternatives to the status quo that are highly innovative, creatively destructive, always in flux, and work best when they facilitate widespread sharing. I would add that shadow systems can also piggyback on existing unstable attractors that the current system tolerates but which have considerable disruptive potential. An example is a high-school-based sustainability project I have been involved with for several years at Western Springs College in central Auckland that functions rather like a shadow system.[101] For starters, it runs as a network in which students, teachers, parents, and environmental facilitators from the local council regularly meet to exchange ideas, but not to approve projects, which come primarily from student-led teams. Projects come and go. Some are 'successful' – like a new waste management system that has diverted 73 per cent of waste from landfill; others die a quiet death – like an attempt to get the school's email signature to include a suggestion not to print the email.[102] Some flare up, create new conversations and then fade away again – like a litter reduction challenge that also raised money to protect the endangered Maui's dolphin.[103]

The network is viewed favourably by the school's senior management team because, while it is constantly advocating change to usual practice – and is therefore an irritant to the status quo – it is also aligned with unstable attractors that are compatible with the values of those in charge. The school wants to support students taking leadership on socially progressive issues, and it wants its systems to reflect cutting-edge sustainability practice. These values sit somewhat uneasily alongside the almighty stable attractor of performance in nationwide assessments and exams. If there is an external exam at stake, sustainability automatically takes second place. This sidelining does not happen through an authoritarian decree, but because we all 'just know' that students must not be allowed to sacrifice their academic performance for other school activities. Nevertheless, over a period of several years this shadow system has grown. More people, more often, are exposed to opportunities to participate. Gradually, disposable cutlery is disappearing from the school, vegetable gardens have sprung up, and students take it for granted that full waste separation is normal. Even more importantly, the students and staff involved are learning that systems *can change* if they are persistent and work together.

––◦––◦––◦––

From an infinite game perspective, every finite game is always on probation. It earns its place not by its size, but by the extent to which it enriches the broader network of infinite values. In the long term, this is what happens anyway. Even the biggest social structure will eventually crumble if it is incompatible with how life works. However, the world in which we live is rife with games that are constantly being shored up, not because they are the best we can do, but because they *are* what we do.

Such games keep expanding and replicating. If you look around, you will see numerous such games – games that exist because they have worked their way into multiple facets of our lives; like distended, throbbing organs that push nutrients bonded with junk through their far-reaching blood vessels.

If you are on the periphery of a system, you may be able to make use of your relative flexibility and work on shadow systems that nudge these monoliths towards more humane practices or that demonstrate different ways of being. Shadow systems may be more effective if they piggyback on the strange attractors that are already challenging current practice such as climate change, recognition that wealth has become too concentrated, the threat of massive species extinction, or an increasing sense that consumption isn't as fun as promised. Network thinking helps us accept that widespread change cannot be designed, forced, or controlled. But we can sow playing fields that bring infinite values into the present, and prepare new fields that will be ready and waiting when the old ones fall apart.

10. Diversity versus sameness

The infinite game tends towards diversity;
Finite games tend towards sameness

Anyone who has travelled must have noticed and, if you are like me, been shocked and saddened by the sameness that has taken over the human world. Shopping malls are almost identical in every country I have recently visited: New Zealand, Australia, the USA, Canada, the UK, the Netherlands. They sell the same products: clothes, shoes, sports paraphernalia, bags, jewellery, stationery, coffee. And those products are largely produced by the same brands: Gap, The Body Shop, Michael Hill (a rare New Zealand export), McDonald's, Starbucks.

This sameness is the product of finite games in which early winners are encouraged to grow and replicate. It is extraordinarily difficult to find a space in the face of their dominance and almost impossible to become one of them. Big fast-food companies and Massive Open Online Courses operate in this way. In agriculture, a few cultivars dominate our major crops such as wheat and rice. We even have an abundance of generalist birds as the niches of specialist species have been destroyed by our charge towards monotony.[104]

Sameness is ultimately fragile. It creates cumbersome, slow-moving entities that don't respond easily to new circumstances. For a while these entities dominate, but eventually too much is compromised and new life bursts through. This breakthrough is highly disruptive if the system it overturns covers much of the territory we inhabit. These sprawling landscapes of sameness are also mind-numbingly, soul-destroyingly oppressive in the here and now. We must not fall into the trap of thinking we must protect them because of the disruption that change will cause.

Diversity is the way of the infinite game, as it is the way of all rich, vibrant and healthy regenerating complex systems.[105] When the opportunity exists, people find niches and fill them with activity that suits that particular niche. They adapt and respond to the life around them, feeding it and being fed by it. One powerful setting for seeing this process in play is cities that have managed to hold on to their vitality and uniqueness. A writer that has captured the thriving city in vivid detail is Jane Jacobs, who undertook detailed observations of American cities in the 1960s.[106] She claimed that 'exuberant diversity' in urban settings is the result of a variety of buildings and spaces that can be used for multiple purposes and a dense concentration of people living close to the street. It is also essential that activities are interconnected, so people move from one interesting feature to another, rather than feeling compelled to travel quickly through dead streets to arrive at their desired destination. Importantly, these settings are not planned in the usual sense. Rather, they evolve from the individual components. That is, if spaces are adaptable and multiple people are encouraged to make an impression on those spaces, diversity will occur. As she puts it:[107]

The ballet of the good city sidewalk never repeats itself from place to place, and in any one place it is always replete with new improvisations.

If, on the other hand, spaces are controlled by a few dominant structures (often the same ones found in the neighbouring suburb and beyond), then, as Jacobs notes, the 'Great Blight of Dullness' will flourish. This leads 'residents to isolate themselves from each other to a fantastic degree', and interchange to become stilted and cautious.[108] Life now exists elsewhere.

Ironically, in a predominantly dull landscape, the locations that manage to retain the diversity that enlivens and inspires us become sites that non-residents visit from afar, which may compromise the life force that made them attractive in the first place. An example of this gravitational pull happens in the build-up to Christmas on a steep residential street in the adjacent suburb to my own. Several years ago, the residents of Franklin Road in Freemans Bay started putting up Christmas lights, until most houses had at least a few lights and some had magnificent displays with Santa and reindeers and train sets that played 'We wish you a Merry Christmas'. Every house was different. At first, this attracted locals who would walk up and down the hill admiring the displays. After a while, however, people started to come from further afield. The last time I went, Franklin Road was clogged with cars as droves of people seeking a little Christmas spirit smothered this flicker of creativity in carbon monoxide fumes.

You see, the odd pocket of something new and different in a city isn't enough. It will either be swamped like Franklin Road, or if there is money to be made, it will be bought, replicated and eventually lose its poetry. In a city that was playing the infinite game, diversity would spring from the 'new improvisations' that Jacobs referred to. That is, from settings in which life wasn't bound up and gagged by same-old institutions but had the freedom to create and re-create itself.

—◦—◦—◦—

It is clear then that the diverse network which characterises the infinite game is in creative tension with the finite game push towards large entities that tend towards replication. While some standardisation based on core values is extremely useful – I would not want to abolish New Zealand's minimum wage or our Human Rights Act for example – too often standardisation serves to concentrate power in a few hands, or reduce the energy and beauty of diversity for the sake of bureaucratic efficiency. I suggest you look carefully at the games in your world and observe how standardisation plays out. Which rules offer standardisation that helps people 'do the right thing'? Which produce standardisation that prevents diversity and feeds a Great Blight of Dullness and despondency?

As infinite players, we should also be cautious about aiming for solutions that can be 'scaled up', as if solutions are only worthwhile when they can be stamped onto as many contexts as possible. This is to tragically overlook people's desire to contribute to their own solutions and the strength of diversity. If instead of thinking in terms of scaling up, we create communities of interest and good lines of communication, people will learn from each other and apply rules to themselves as collectives. Some solutions will be scaled up, but it is so much more *lifelike* if they come out of the community itself, rather than from an external edict.

Importantly, too, communities of interest allow a range of solutions to co-exist. These provide those delicious sensations of reawakening that come from variety in the here and now, as well as multiple tributaries leading to the future. Sameness is ultimately weak, and sets the stage for systems collapse. Diversity is ultimately strong and sets the stage for resilience. If it wasn't part of the problem, we might be grateful that the status quo is so same old, same old. It's one of its fatal flaws.

11. Awe versus control

Infinite players are in awe of life in all its forms; Finite players attempt to control the life forms relevant to the game

When I was a young adult and unhappy with myself and the world, one of the places I found respite was by the ocean. The coasts I loved were wild. They had waves smashing on black rocks and long stretches of sand reaching into the distance. I especially liked grey, misty days, the ones that kept other people away. On such days, I could walk for hours and see almost no one. On those desolate beaches, of which New Zealand has many, I was able to feel the relief of my own insignificance. Instead of my personal drama being the centre of all things, it became, which it *is* from almost any perspective other than my own, a mere blip in the story of life. No matter what happened, the endless pounding of the waves on the shore would continue. It was a bit like the scene in the movie *Planet of the Apes* (1968) where Taylor, the astronaut hero, finds the remnants of the Statue of Liberty buried in the sand of a lonely beach. We sure can make a mess of it, but life, in some form or other, goes on.

Strangely, however, after allowing my own drama to recede into the mist of the coast, I would also often feel a new sense of possibility. Those walks were when I would dream big, imagining what I could create and become. I would stop every so often and gaze out across the sea while mental mirages of possible personal futures appeared. Niki the lawyer, Niki the diplomat, Niki the mother, super-slim Niki with long hair, silver loop earrings and a flowing batik dress like the cool girls. Now I swear that no one ever told me to 'go lose and find yourself in nature', but my experience of doing exactly that is so common as to almost be a truism.[109] There is something about those places we experience as wild that blows us away and then invites us to rethink ourselves.

—o—o—o—

Nature is the backdrop to all our games, and the infinite player inside us senses this. When we are far from people or the signs they leave behind, it is not just that we reconnect with the beauty and magnificence of our planet, but we also feel free of human constraint.[110] We catch a glimpse of what it might be to start over, without the tedium of working our way through the innumerable rules of our society.

George Monbiot describes a fascinating case illustrating the appeal of societies in which people are relatively free to explore the natural world in his book *Feral: Searching for Enchantment on the Frontiers of Rewilding*.[111] It concerns the early period of European settlement in

North America. The Europeans brought with them many of the ways of their homeland including cumbersome clothes and agricultural practices. The Native Americans lived as they had for centuries – able to move within vast natural domains that were largely outside human control. On occasion, Europeans and Native Americans ended up living in each other's communities. Sometimes this was the result of European children being kidnapped by Native American tribes, or of Native American children being brought up by Europeans. When children who had experienced both cultures were given the choice of where to live they *consistently* chose the Native American community. Hector de Crèvecoeur observed that kidnapped European children wanted to stay with their captors because, the children claimed, this way of life provided 'the most perfect freedom, the ease of living, the absence of those cares and corroding solicitudes which so often prevail with us'.[112] The problem of young men defecting from colonial settlements to Native American tribes in the early 1600s was apparently so great that, if captured, they were put to death.

What Monbiot's case shows is that 'civilisation' may protect us from some of the known dangers out there, but it does this by putting a layer between us and the natural world. This layer can be immensely dispiriting at a personal level. Society's games are always a slightly uncomfortable fit, even the good ones. Every so often, we need somewhere to step outside them.

—o—o—o—

Not only is the natural world a setting in which we can temporarily feel free from the finite games that haunt us, but nature's vastness and complexity gives our human games endless unpredictability. We cannot, and will never, 'control' nature.[113] To imagine this is possible is like imagining a two-year-old child successfully running for secretary-general of the United Nations. Infinite players accept this. No, it is more: infinite players *delight in* this. A society that saw nature in this way would retain awe for other species and the biosphere in which we are embedded. Another way of putting this is that an infinite game perspective nurtures eco-centric environmentalism; an environmentalism founded on a love of nature for its own sake.[114]

Many Westerners do consider the natural world of value for its own sake. Nature stirs us in such a way that we *just know* it matters – recall the infinite values word cloud in Chapter One (see p. 38). But in our highly industrialised and urbanised societies we can lose sight of this attachment. As put by Paul Watson of Sea Shepherd, an activist group that draws attention to the plight of marine life:[115]

> We must develop a philosophy where a redwood tree is more sacred than a human-made religious icon, where a species of bird or butterfly is of more value and deserving of more respect than the crown jewels of a nation, and where the survival of a species of cacti or flower is more important than the survival of a monument to human conceit like the pyramids.

Because, as Watson implies here, the tree, the bird and the flower are precious and irreplaceable in a way that can't be matched by artefacts produced by people. We may be hard-pressed to find the kind of deep respect for the natural world Watson is advocating in current Western institutional structures (as opposed to in many people's hearts and personal practices – where it is often alive and well), but it is less elusive in the structures of indigenous communities.[116] In these cultures there is often an intimate relationship between the patterns of the natural world and the human world, with the latter seeming to stem from the former.[117] Earlier I referred to Elizabeth Thomas's observations of the apparent understanding between the Ju/wa people and the lions they shared their environment with (see p. 35). Similarly, according to the Australian depth psychologist David Tacey, Australian Aborigines 'felt' the environment to be part of themselves and to be alive with spirits and forces. He argues that modern Australians, however, occupy a landscape that is seen as a 'dead objective background to our busy, ego-centred and self-propelling lives'.[118] In a similar vein, the ecopsychologist Bill Plotkin has written that a 'mystic affiliation' with the 'wild world' is 'the very core of maturity, and it is precisely what mainstream Western society has overlooked – or actively suppressed and expelled'.[119]

Whether or not your worldview encompasses the possibility of a landscape that is alive with spirits and forces, it is undeniable that the natural world is operating at every level and in every moment. Not only do we eat and breathe it, but we have porous skin and ears and eyes that take in what is around us. Our bodies are full of bacteria. We humans are complex systems: both as individuals and as societies we are profoundly and *permanently* interwoven with the non-human world. That the natural world cannot be fully bent to our desire is, to many of us, exhilarating. The infinite human game knows that it is tiny in the face of whatever nature is up to.

—◦—◦—◦—

Finite games, on the other hand, attempt to control the life forms relevant to the game. An implicit assumption of such games is that nature is akin to a shopping mall where we can take what we like, as long as we have figured out a way to pay for it and get it home. We plough through the Brazilian Cerrado with its 32 endangered animal species and 44 unique plant species in order to make way for soybeans.[120] We cut down Indonesian rainforest to plant palm oil, threatening the habitat of orang-utans and contributing massively to carbon dioxide in the atmosphere.[121] Here in New Zealand we convert thousands of hectacres of land to intensive dairy farming, leading to polluted rivers and threatened water tables. And, in every Western city, we get out chainsaws, cranes and concrete mixers to pave paradise with apartment blocks and parking lots, squeezing out biodiversity as we go.

These actions are possible because of our capacity to turn our backs on the larger implications of our actions and set our sights on winning the game at hand. In New Zealand, challenging the sustainability of intensive dairying is somewhat analogous to challenging support for 'our troops' in the USA. Farmers, as I learnt growing up, are the 'backbone' of our country, and in recent years we have shifted away from sheep, beef cattle and pigs and towards dairy cows.[122] We are the world's largest exporter of dairy products with 95 per cent of our production going overseas.

In response to the call for feedback on New Zealand's proposal to the 2015 Paris climate conference, a group of us at the University of Auckland wrote a submission urging ambitious greenhouse gas emissions targets. As 48 per cent of New Zealand's emissions come from agriculture, and dairying is a significant source of these emissions in the form of methane, we made several suggestions for scaling back intensive dairying.[123] Rodney Hide, a columnist from the country's largest newspaper the *New Zealand Herald*, attacked our submission, accusing us of being a 'Conclave' while dairy farmers 'face facts about how the world works' including 'the economics of what milk costs and what milk returns'.[124]

Hide's reaction to our questioning of dairying is a classic illustration of the finite game playing that keeps so many environmentally destructive practices alive. The game, he is saying, is about money. This implies that it is irrelevant what making that money costs in terms of the life systems of our planet, because money is more important than all that. Money is 'how the world works'. Money, as you know and I know and Rodney Hide knows full well too, is actually only how the exchange of many (certainly not all) goods and services between human beings works. The *world*, on the other hand, responds to the physical reality of our actions. All the signs suggest that if we put large quantities of methane in the atmosphere the planet will warm, regardless of what we declare to be 'the facts'.

In Infinite Game workshops, there is a very interesting change in how the paper darts are treated when the participants move from playing with them in infinite game conditions to finite game conditions. In the first game, when they are asked to keep the darts in play and include everyone who wants to take part, there is always a lot of attention paid to the darts themselves. People inspect the darts closely and watch how they fly. Their main comments to each other concern how well the darts perform *as darts*: 'Wow, that one flies so straight!' 'Look at this one, it's got little flaps on the wings.' 'Oops, that didn't go where I intended!' And so on. When they are told that the object of the game is to win and the winner is the person with the most darts, almost no one cares about the darts as darts. Each dart counts as one dart, no matter how well it flies or how much skill and attention went into making it. The players focus on each other as they look suspiciously at their opponents, attempt negotiations, and clutch on to and count their darts.

This transformation in people's attitude towards the darts is analogous to what happens to nature under finite games that have lost touch with the infinite game. Nature as nature – with its wildness, beauty, mystery and unpredictability – fades away. Instead nature becomes an object to be used as demanded by the game in play.

—o—o—o—

None of this is to say that a society informed by the infinite game would be a passive onlooker in regard to nature, consuming only the bare minimum needed for the survival of our species. That would be to turn our backs on so much of what it is to be people-like, including our curiosity and ingenuity. It would also be an affront to our compassion. Think, for example, of denying young people lifesaving medical treatment on the grounds that it is meddling with nature. Yes, it is meddling with nature, but would we also not plant food, given that farming is sometimes considered the turning point at which people ceased to be in harmony with the rest of nature?

If nature could talk, I think she would say something like: 'People, remember that love lies at the centre of what you consider most precious of all. Use your ingenuity and curiosity to keep that love in play. Look after each other, and, insofar as you are able with your limited vision, be gentle on the rest of the world. Try not to let your care for each other brutalise that which is the foundation of all life, just as you know not to let your care for one part of the human world jeopardise the flourishing of other parts.'

So nature, as I imagine her, would not encourage us to deny our special importance to ourselves. That would be *unnatural*. Even in societies with myths and traditions that knit people to the land, human relationships are still of vital importance.[125] As Eugene Anderson, an anthropologist form the University of California, puts it, most traditional societies are 'split' in relation to nature and 'manage unevenly'.[126] Every human group alters their environment in some way.[127] We are a species with a sense of possibility in relation to the world we live in. We must work with this truth as much as with the truth that our meddling with nature could be the end of us.

—○—○—○—

One of the traditional divides in the push towards human and ecological flourishing appeared right there – in the wording of the first part of this sentence. Many of us veer towards either the human or the ecological side of the equation, and then talk as if they are at odds. I have heard social activists say that it is privileged, indulgent and naïve to put efforts into, say, a Predator Free New Zealand, above efforts to increase social justice. Similarly, environmentalists often talk as if people are the problem and must be brought into line – by behaviour change programmes or legislation that mandates correct practice.

If, on the other hand, we see ourselves in an infinite game that asks us to treasure life both in the here and now and into the future, these sides fade away. I am not arguing that it is impossible to change behaviour or legislate for environmental protection – those approaches can work to meet environmental goals. It seems to me theoretically feasible, for example, that we could reverse climate change under capitalism as usual if we make carbon-free fuels more economically viable and develop and install technologies that extract carbon from the atmosphere. Nor is it impossible to increase social justice while treating nature as a resource. We can, for example, increase material wellbeing for people in poverty (at least in the short term) by continuing to mine the Earth and turn forests into agricultural lands. We probably don't *need* orang-utans or to preserve New Zealand's unique flora and fauna.

The environment versus people debate fades away when the infinite game is in play, because to give up on one or the other is to give up on the depths and richness of life itself. It is almost never the case, for example, that the only way to keep people in work is to pay them to wreck the environment. That is an unimaginative play at best – at worst it is a deliberate attempt to pull apart the people who are attempting to support themselves and their families from those who are attempting to preserve part of the natural world. We should not be taken in by it, let alone offer it ourselves. Environmentalists often need to learn more about how to honour people. And social justice advocates often need to recognise that some people feel a love for wild things and places that is real and human – even as it goes beyond the human sphere. What's more, this love of nature helps keep alive the *awe*-some context in which all our other games are played.

Chapter Four

Knowledge

There are at least three kinds of knowledge. The first concerns the biological and physical world, the second concerns the social world, and the third concerns our inner selves. From an infinite game perspective, knowledge in each of these fields is provisional. A society informed by the infinite game would be very wary indeed of claims that the truth has been discovered and it is embedded in the formula proposed by today's winner. Instead it would be asking: Does this knowledge match the landscape in which we now find ourselves? Does it help us live well together as creatures in awe of life in all its forms? Importantly, *how* we seek knowledge and *what we do* with it is just as relevant to such questions as the content of the knowledge itself. The first section in this chapter will focus on the first two types of knowledge as described above and the second section on the third.

12. Seeking information versus claiming knowledge

The infinite game seeks and responds to information about the world; Winners of finite games claim knowledge of the world which may be treated as the truth

Knowledge of the biological and physical world comes from action, observation, reflection and communication. We know how to treat an abscess because people tried out alternatives, observed the effect, reflected on what they had done and communicated this information to others. In pre-European Māori culture, the juice from roasted harakeke roots was known to help; and in contemporary New Zealand culture, we consider antibiotics useful. Both medicines were derived from essentially the same cycle. Of course, this cycle is infused with numerous assumptions that limit the imagination of knowledge makers and practitioners in both scenarios. In other words, learning is bound within the finite games of the culture concerned. And medicines don't always work, because even the most magnificent of them are just crude human attempts to influence complex biological processes. (But, if you have an abscess, it is always nice to have someone to turn to who at least knows what the problem is.)

Science is this knowledge cycle on steroids. According to one estimate, there are 1.8 million scientific articles published every year.[128] Each of these, in theory at least, shines new light on some feature of the world. Science has brought us frameworks to explain a huge range of phenomena, from the origins of our planet and the species within it, to the structure of living cells and the way elements combine to form molecules. Now, there are many limitations to science. As argued by numerous writers, scientific investigation often involves manipulating or pulling apart life and other natural forms.[129] This can lead to both the destruction of what is being examined – such as when an animal is injected with a toxic substance in order to observe how it responds – and pave the way for even more destruction – if, for example, that toxic substance is then turned into a chemical weapon. Science, after all, plays with the stuff of the Earth, and then releases its findings to whoever is interested. If that does not strike you as at least somewhat dangerous, then you have a lot more confidence in our ability to predict and control the consequences of our tinkering than I do![130]

Science can also be slow to adjust to new information, despite its overall mandate to do just that.[131] Scientists are embedded in human systems, and carry out their work within the demands of finite games such as the methodological rules of rigour that apply to each discipline.

In my experience, many scientists are relatively cautious, following well-established topic lines that lead to ever-more-tiny tributaries. I sometimes let out a huge sigh when I review yet another article that ends with 'more research is needed to establish if . . .' It would be so refreshing to occasionally read instead: 'having got to the end of this project we now realise that this line of investigation is not worth further exploration'.

But no, following the tributaries is a reasonably safe way to win the high-prestige finite game of scientific publishing, so it is very difficult indeed not to play this way even when you strongly suspect it is a dead end (I've certainly done it). As Paul Erhlich, a well-known ecologist who focuses on population issues, has written about his own field, 'the literature is clogged with dribs and drabs of information on a vast variety of organisms and communities – increasingly sophisticated studies of more and more trivial problems'.[132] It's science's version of economic growth for the sake of economic growth – research growth for the sake of research growth. Scientists (or their fans) also get irritating if they imply that science is The Answer to human problems. This slips into idolatry and the finite play of interest here: a claim to be the holder of The Truth.

Despite these caveats, scientific insights are extremely compelling. If there is a scientific explanation for a specific natural phenomenon – say, how carbon cycles between the soil, plants, animals, the oceans and the atmosphere – it seems very unlikely to me that a more satisfying explanation is held elsewhere in the store of human knowledge. Although I do not understand the vast majority of scientific insights, I do understand the principles of observation, mathematical reasoning, and so on, upon which they are based. Scientific claims are discoverable – that is, they can be traced back to empirical observations or stated first principles. There are, or should be, no stopping points in scientific discussions at which a good scientist simply claims to 'get' something that is beyond reason or observation. Good science involves constant attempts to articulate meaningful knowledge in forms that make sense to others; and constant recognition that this knowledge is always partial and subject to adjustment.

So science helps us understand the biological and physical world, and a society informed by the infinite game would welcome scientific perspectives on issues related to these domains. Furthermore, it would respond to scientific discoveries about the world. It would, for example, tweak our current finite games given the scientific consensus on climate change. I regularly go to talks where I must sit through a safety briefing on what to do in the event of a fire or earthquake – an event of minuscule likelihood – while our global system continues to put the environment we depend on at great peril. From an infinite game perspective, absurdities like this can be understood as blockages caused by overvaluing finite games that refuse to adjust to new realities. Fire drills can be absorbed within our current games. An adequate response to climate change, it would seem, cannot.

—◦—◦—◦—

Knowledge of each other – the social world – follows the same process of action, observation, reflection and communication as knowledge of the natural world. Undoubtedly, much can be learnt about people from academic scholarship, including history, philosophy, psychology, sociology and anthropology. These understandings give us some general principles to chew over, and, as with science, they are fascinating pursuits if you are so inclined. Indeed, this book includes much academic scholarship of this type. Social science and the humanities are, however, working at an extra level of complexity to the natural sciences.

This is because human societies are embedded *within* the natural world, but can't be *fully explained* by that world. Jared Diamond gives an interesting example of the interplay between natural and social phenomena in his book *Collapse: How Societies Choose to Fail or Survive*, where he compares the Dominican Republic and Haiti.[133] This example illustrates the complexity involved in attempting to understand social systems. The Dominican Republic and Haiti occupy the same island of Hispaniola, and yet, as Diamond explains, have developed very differently. As he puts it: 'From an airplane flying high overhead, the border looks like a sharp line with bends, cut arbitrarily across the island by a knife, and abruptly dividing a darker and greener landscape east of the line (the Dominican side) from a paler and browner landscape west of the line (the Haitian side).[134] Part of the difference in development is likely due to higher rainfall in the Dominican Republic, and hence better growing conditions. In addition, however, the two countries have experienced differing historical conditions, and these, according to Diamond, are crucial to the current divergence in their landscapes.

As Diamond explains, while the Spanish were the initial colonisers of Hispaniola in the 1500s, their interest was focused on their mainline settlements. This enabled French settlers to take over the western side of the island, bringing with them people from Africa to be their slaves, and developing sugar plantations. At the end of the 1700s, some of the Africans brought to Hispaniola rose in revolt and eventually succeeded in expelling the French rulers, creating the country of Haiti on the western side of the island in 1804. By then, Haiti carried a large population which has continued to grow, putting pressure on the soils and leading to deforestation due to the demand for land and the need for charcoal as a fuel. Meanwhile, the less populous eastern region eventually re-established its identity as a Spanish colony. European settlers arrived and the Dominican Republic developed as a trading nation. As the world was industrialising, the Dominican Republic was able to generate hydro-electric power from its rivers, which along with a ban on commercial logging in the 1960s, enabled it to retain sizeable areas of forest. Hence from the air Haiti looks pale brown and the Dominican Republic looks dark green.

As of November 2015, according to the Global Finance website, the Dominican Republic ranked eighty-sixth in wealth amongst the world's 180 nations and Haiti one hundred and sixty-sixth.[135] The former country also annually emits 2.03 metric tons of CO_2 per capita, and the latter 0.30 metric tons (New Zealand, by way of comparison, emits 6.74 metric tons per capita and the USA 15.53).[136] It is difficult to pinpoint the key factors which have influenced the history of any human group – the above is a massive simplification of Diamond's analysis, which is itself a simplification – and impossible to pinpoint exactly why events occurred as they did. Why, for example, did people enslaved in the west of

Hispaniola revolt against those who kept them captive, when enslaved people in other parts of the Americas did not revolt – or at least their revolts did not gather momentum? It took the African-Haitians thirteen years to oust the French, during which time many tens of thousands of them died. That is an incredible story of persistence.

So as the history of Hispaniola illustrates, knowledge of the social world must take account of the natural world, but introduces additional variables that considerably complicate the story we are telling. And when we study and describe the social world, we are describing ourselves. This all means that what we come up with in the social sciences can't be applied in the same way as discoveries made by the natural sciences.

Climate change, for example, is a relatively simple problem in relation to its physics, chemistry, biology and ecology. This is not to say it can be predicted or is fully understood, but given licence to do so, scientists can provide precise advice right now on technologies and practices that could probably prevent large temperature rises over the next century.[137]

However, social scientists cannot provide correspondingly precise advice on how to get societies to actually implement the changes necessary. This is not so much because we lack imagination but because we cannot stand outside ourselves as social actors and make it happen. All social scholars can do is take a position as players. This means looking for allies and trying to veer the social debate towards our best collective knowledge about the natural world, the patterns and possibilities we have observed in human societies, and our understanding of what people need to flourish. Others will almost certainly take counter-positions and events outside the game will facilitate or disrupt its course. The 'outcome' (to the extent that it is meaningful to talk of an outcome) is unpredictable. And crucially, from an infinite game perspective, having experts dream up and impose their ideal social world on the rest of us would violate the fundamental principle that everyone gets to play the game of how we organise ourselves. It would be to claim that we are the holders of truth and all must bow to our god.

–◦–◦–◦–

Formal scholarship is not the only source of knowledge about ourselves. Another form of knowledge with huge value in making us aware of what we have created and what we could create in our lives together is art. Essentially, art observes and communicates what it is to be human and to live in community.[138] It does this through stories, songs, paintings and dance that exaggerate experiences so they are more intense and pure than the original. As put by Alain de Botton: 'Valuable elements may be easier to experience in art . . . than in reality.'[139] If you want to understand the power of communities recognising each other's humanity, for example, you will learn a lot by watching *Pride*, a 2014 film about a lesbian and gay group supporting Welsh coal miners during the 1984 strike in the UK.[140] Films like *Pride* cut to the chase – they show us the prejudice, fear, warmth, shame and secrecy of people trying to make lives in a world not set up for them. By simplifying life, they help us focus on its underlying drivers.

Through its beauty, art also draws our attention at a sensory level. Beauty, as noted by the ecopsychologist Laura Sewell who studies visual processes, is a 'feast [for] our neurons – our senses now enlivened, attentive and synchronized'.[141] This means we pay attention and absorb what we are experiencing on a different level to intellectual arguments. The Australian depth psychologist Peter Dicker calls the ability of aesthetic, artistic works to express human experience a 'poetic eloquence' that can 'reveal nature to us'.[142] The learning that happens through art is a 'soft' process. It does not and cannot barrage us with logic and evidence, so instead it lays in front of us a picture of the world, and invites us to respond.

Art also lies at the heart of the myths and symbols we live by.[143] These are not constrained by the linear rules and rigid processes of academic scholarship. While the transparency of scholarship in general and science in particular is one of its strengths, the evasiveness of mythology is one of *its* strengths. Unlike scientific ways of knowing, myths and symbols assume an active, intuitive receiver who 'gets it' without necessarily being able to articulate what has been 'got'. The most powerful of such symbols reach into the depths of human experience, and present them in a narrative or other form that resonates with the spirt of the times in which we are living. As Joseph Campbell, who has written several books on mythology, puts it, myths use local materials and are derived from 'an architecture unconsciously dictated from within'.[144] Due to the way in which they reverberate through people – both as individuals and groups – myths have, as noted by the theologian Lloyd Geering, 'helped people to feel at home on the Earth'.[145]

A fascinating suggestion by James P. Carse in his book *The Religious Case Against Belief* is that myths and other symbols are in fact powerful to the extent that they are *not* fully coherent.[146] This is because an incomplete or somewhat contradictory story has room for interpretation and discussion – we can and must bring it alive. If this is the case, then a text like the Bible is not weakened by its many factual contradictions (for example, God told Noah to take both two – Genesis 6:19, 20 – and seven – Genesis 7:2 – pairs of animals on the Ark) and ambiguities (for example, 'The LORD is a man of war' – Exodus 15:3; 'Now the God of peace be with you all' – Romans 15:33). These inconsistencies are instead essential to the Bible's lifeblood. They are what enable people who identify with Christian mythology to rise above the Bible's details and feel drawn into a profound conversation that is both ancient and enduring.

Shakespeare is a secular example of similar appeal. His plays can be terribly difficult for a modern audience and don't contain clear arguments. But there is something about hearing or speaking a familiar, clever line – 'The lady doth protest too much, methinks' – a line that has previously reverberated through thousands of theatres, which can draw us into a sense of lively commonality with each other.[147]

So, as vehicles for moving forward together, art, symbols and myths give people a foothold that helps us recognise each other's humanity and that reflects and simplifies the core issues we face. That is one of the reasons that this book has a symbol at its core. The infinite game is highly resonant well beyond the particular principles I have written about here. You either 'get it' or you don't. And 'getting it' does not mean understanding or agreeing with it exactly, so much as sensing in it a capacity to explore what matters. And exploring what matters is what the infinite game is all about.

—◇—◇—◇—

The novelist Ursula K. Le Guin wrote: 'Truth can go out of stories, you know. What was true becomes meaningless, even a lie, because the truth has gone into another story. The water of the spring rises in another place.'[148] From an infinite game perspective, this insight applies to every finite game constructed on the basis of our knowledge of the world and each other. The truth of these games is provisional. Importantly, this is not because certain facts shift from being correct to incorrect, or because values change. It is because any finite game is only true insofar as it is genuinely holding and conveying what we know to be the best match, or at least an adequate match, between our understanding of the world and what we most value. At one time, for example, it was true that petrochemical fertilisers increased crop yields. Now, the truth has moved to the effects of these fertilisers on surrounding ecosystems and the social ramifications of large-scale agri-business. It was also once true that the USA was a democracy because all (well, never *all*) adults were able to vote. Now there is doubt as to whether the USA is still a democracy – that is, whether the voting process actually captures what people want – because of the layers of constraint politicians face in being able to speak authentically.

All societies must make decisions about how to interact with the natural world and how to best organise ourselves. An infinite game approach encourages decisions based on a truth that is 'the best for now as far as we can tell'. It would resist setting these truths in stone and instead promote science and arts that are attuned to what we need to know next.

—o—o—o—

So how does this view of seeking and responding to information resonate with, and offer approaches for, those of us attempting to contribute to the common good? First, it highlights how important it is to bring new, *interesting*, knowledge to the attention of society. (Dull knowledge produced by being trapped in the research-production game doesn't cut it.) This is often the central focus of the scholars and artists in our midst. Second, it points to the importance of humility in the face of all knowledge. This includes the knowledge we hold as scientists or social researchers which, while sometimes useful, may be revered beyond its due. Not only may we sometimes be wrong in a factual sense, but most knowledge is only powerful insofar as it works its way into public discourse. We can know, and be right in knowing, but this alone does not do the trick.

This brings me to the third point: we can advocate for the *particular* knowledge we hold to be given a hearing, but, in the long term, we also need to advocate for social systems that are more generally responsive to observation and analysis. This could be another finite game: the game in which we bring in the scientists and artists and philosophers and ask them what they see happening in the world and how we should respond in light of their insights. It should not, of course, be up to them what we do next, but to ignore the makers of new knowledge is very reckless indeed.

13. Understanding versus training

Infinite players attempt to understand themselves;
Finite players attempt to train themselves

If you want to learn how to win one of the many finite games available in the Western world, you need to train yourself. For example, to get an A+ in an introductory psychology exam at most universities I know of, by far the best strategy is to learn the theories and examples given in the lectures and the textbook and to ensure you can paraphrase these adequately. You should also learn the critiques of these theories. You take a great risk if you critique them from your own perspective, as your critique is likely to look naïve to an examiner. This is partly because you are given a crude version of the theory to play with and so you may draw attention to a problem that only exists in that version and not in the theory itself. It is also partly because you don't yet know the discipline's rules of critique. The rules are too complicated to explain here, but they are *not* to reflect on incoming information from your current knowledge base and describe how that information extends your understanding or contradicts what you think to be the case.

This is a process of training because the aim is to replicate a pre-determined model of the A+ exam. Creativity is an inhibitor rather than facilitator of the process. Training is also the quickest way to a place in a ballet company, winning a national title in swimming, or selling real estate. There are formulas available and you are much more likely to win if you learn and apply them. As we turn more of life into finite games, we also offer more training programmes. You can, for example, obtain a certificate in Animal Management (with Canine Behaviour or Captive Wild Animals specialities), Liaison Interpreting, or Community Skills from the technical institute down the road from me.

Training produces the sameness discussed in the previous chapter. Sometimes sameness is its explicit aim, as in ballet where every move is precisely prescribed right down to the arrangement of the fingers. Sometimes it is implicit, as in psychology exams that steer students away from deep engagement and towards an exemplar that the skilled can reproduce. The effect of training is that the same knowledge is held by more and more players, not that more and more people are concerned with how to improve the underpinning project and its contribution to helping us live well together.

Of course, training can contribute to keeping the infinite game in play. I love that ballet does not change. It respects the dance community that came before us, and allows us to honour their skill at creating lovely human lines. I also think it is good for psychology students to learn a selection of past theories and be able to paraphrase them. Without some common discipline, it is difficult to have rich conversations with each other. But if we are concerned with the infinite game, this training should not be allowed to take over. Instead, we need to leave room for people to understand themselves.

Understanding is used here to mean a capacity for self-reflection that takes into account one's feelings and the effect of one's actions on the world at large. When we are caught in finite games, our feelings may be ignored and we are encouraged to focus on the effect of our actions in relation to the game at hand. Traditional academia, for example, requires the ability to override boredom, and, strangely, to override curiosity – it is important not to become distracted by the French colonists' enthusiasm for slavery when you are supposed to be putting together a brief history of Haiti. A real estate agent may be shocked at first to realise that she must push parties into offering more or taking less than they feel comfortable with, but after a while she learns to keep her feelings in check and do the pushing. These strategies work to win the academic or real estate selling games.

Paying attention to one's feelings, on the other hand, holds finite games to account. The story of seventeen-year-old Sarah Harriet Thomas, who was hanged outside a Bristol jail on 20 April 1849 for the murder of her employer, illustrates this point. Here is a newspaper account at the time:[149]

> This wretched criminal underwent the sentence of the law, for the murder of her mistress, on Friday. The scaffold was erected over the great gates of the gaol. Between twelve and one o'clock in the morning she partook of a mutton chop; she afterwards laid down. The chaplain arrived at seven o'clock, and she seemed more attentive than before to her religious duties. Half an hour previous to the execution the governor of the gaol, Mr. Gardiner, announced to her the painful duty which he had to perform, and said he hoped she would accompany him to the place of execution quietly. She stamped with her foot several times and said she would not go. She seemed almost frantic, and at the time appointed, Mr. Gardiner was compelled to procure the assistance of six or seven men, who led her into the press-yard. She resisted all the time . . . After having been pinioned she walked without assistance as far as the drop, but afterwards she was obliged to be led up the ladder by two of the turnkeys. She struggled violently, and shrieked in a dreadful manner.

A BBC retrospective on the event noted that 'so great and moving was the awful scene that even the prison governor was so overcome that he fainted', and that 'a great many of the crowd felt repulsed by what they had seen and many carried the memory of that grisly day for years afterwards'.[150] Sarah Thomas was, perhaps as a result of her emotive display, the last woman to be hanged in Bristol. The point here is that in an absolutely direct and forthright manner, Sarah Thomas understood and acted on her urge to live and declared herself unwilling to play nicely. She 'made a fuss'. And in doing so she exposed the brutality of public executions.[151]

It is hard to overemphasise the extent to which we are obliged to control our feelings in order to be taken seriously as finite players. As a woman with leadership roles in a university setting, I have learnt to speak slowly and clearly and assert myself in conversations at meetings. I have also learnt not to sacrifice my own voice for the sake of enabling others. These actions have an emotional cost to me, as they turn me away from my more compassionate self that looks out for those who cannot quite find the moment to join in. I am not proud of becoming this way, and wish I had the imagination to be strong and sure and compassionate all at once, rather than just behave as I have seen the powerful players do. But at least I have not forgotten what it feels like to be on the outer; and in the meetings that I run, I use many strategies to encourage people to participate as they are.

—o—o—o—

If we paid closer attention to the infinite game, we would, as a society, also actively encourage self-understanding and personal reflection. We would see maturity as the capacity to notice and adjust our behaviour in light of our feelings and the impact of our behaviour on others. Being well trained to win one of the finite games on offer would be celebrated for what it is – a useful skill in some cases, but always partial. I often wonder what would happen if we held a day on which everyone was encouraged to make a fuss. Along with obvious moves such as children refusing to go inside when the bell signals that playtime is over, my fantasy is that the CEOs of our major corporations would stamp their feet and complain that they are tired of having to put the bottom line in front of workers' conditions. There are not necessarily any real winners of finite games – a truth we may overlook in the assumption that 'they' (the holders of power), unlike 'us' (those without power), have found a sweet spot in which their values and their work are in complete harmony.

Attending to our feelings is also vital when we advocate for the good society. We can certainly train people in the skills which we feel are needed to progress the issues in our domain – be they gardening, letter writing, non-violent direct action, computer modelling, or counting birds. But unless we also allow people to grow themselves and their relationships with each other in an accepting, tolerant environment, we run the risk of producing emotionally inflexible robots. I am not suggesting that we all indulge in endless emotional avalanches in which every impulse is acted upon. Nor am I suggesting that we get caught up in popular emotional discourses – like being 'stressed' – which are often used to avoid closer consideration of what is really going on.[152]

I am simply suggesting that we always remember the importance of people being able to be people-like. If people can't be people-like when they are attempting to create the good life, then what, exactly, are we doing it all for?

Chapter Five

Time

The final domain is time. Finite games treat time as a foe, to be held captive for as long as possible. In the infinite game, time is like a roll of the dice. It is the hand of luck, the great unknown that brings anticipation and excitement.

14. Looking to the future versus replicating the past

The infinite game looks to the future and does not
assume the past will reoccur; In finite games players
try to replicate the winning strategies of the past

Having argued in the previous chapter that life would be a lot more interesting if we stamped our feet in protest when asked to go against our desire to fully live, in this chapter I argue that to play the infinite game well, we need to come to terms with death. This is not a contradiction, but an understanding that life feeds on death in a million guises including cornflakes, baby gazelles, bankruptcy, revolutions, retirement, and sites abandoned due to radioactivity. Sometimes, to enable life, it is our turn to step aside. As the developmental psychologist Erik Erikson wrote: 'Healthy children will not fear life if their elders have integrity enough not to fear death.'[153] If we do not fear death, or at least do not set up games that attempt to preserve old life at any cost, then new life, that which is itching to be expressed, has a chance. In these circumstances, the future – change whose form is yet to be seen – is possible.

–○–○–○–

From a finite game perspective, on the other hand, the realisation that life will end for each of us individually, and in due course for our entire species, is often considered unspeakably dreadful. It is almost as if simply entertaining the idea is dangerous, alerting death to our presence and implying that we are here for the taking.[154] Instead, we are supposed to be on the lookout for eternal life. At the individual level, there are a myriad of options that promise to keep us going indefinitely – or at least staving off death until we are really, really old. Longevity (or immortality), we are told, requires worshipping this god, eating this food, not eating this other food, taking these high-priced pills, following this philosophy, meditating in this style, or adhering to some other magical practice.

The search for eternal life immediately constructs a finite game with the power to obliterate us if we dare disobey. If you could live forever, you would be almost obliged to throw everything at making that happen: any other goal pales in comparison. Such a quest profoundly distracts us from our roles as infinite players. There is no remaining space for our collective wellbeing, or even for spontaneous self-expression. Instead we must follow the rules that will ensure we live forever.

The finite game of avoiding death works the same way at the species level. When we are told that climate change, the collapse of our economic system, or a superbug is threatening to annihilate us, and that we can stop this, the corollary is that there is no alternative but to try with all our might to avoid this abrupt end to human life. If, for example, climate change is truly 'it', then it is mere squeamishness to worry about what may result from fighting climate change with all we've got. So what if we end up with nuclear waste, oceans swarming with jellyfish, or dim skies full of sulphur, at least we are still here!

Coming to terms with death means accepting that life will end, and that focusing wholeheartedly on the latest edicts for keeping this end at bay is, ultimately, a hollow game.[155] The alternative is to make this the best game we can, for as long as it lasts. An essay by Tony Kushner called 'Despair is a lie we tell ourselves' captures this magnificently. At the beginning of the essay the writer is told by a taxi driver that there is a supernova 60 light years away, destined to wipe out the Earth. The essay then goes on to describe the more likely ways in which we will be 'got', including global warming, the collapse of our economic system, or a catastrophic war, and urges people to play a part in solving these problems. At the end of the essay, Kushner writes:[156]

So when the supernova comes to get us we don't want to be disappointed in ourselves. We should hope to be able to say proudly to the supernova, that angel of death, 'Hello supernova, we have been expecting you, we know all about you, because in our schools we teach science not creationism, and so we have been expecting you, everywhere everyone has been expecting you, except Texas. And we would like to say, supernova, in the moment before we are returned by your protean fire to our previous inchoate state, clouds of incandescent atomic vapour, we'd like to declare that we have tried our best and worked hard to make a good and just and free and peaceful world, a world that is better for our having been here, at least we believe it is.'

Now *that* is an infinite play. It is not a suggestion to give up on what we know enables human life now or in the future, but it is a reminder to keep the fact of our existence in perspective. Existence *per se* is neither the point, nor, ultimately, is it in our control. Sometimes in the talks and workshops I have given on my book *Psychology for a Better World* that focus on inspiring people to get involved in social action, people ask me if the strategies I am advocating are 'enough' to prevent widespread disaster. It is as if they want me, as a psychologist, to provide a sure-fire way to get people to fully realise the dangers we face as a species and act consistently with this realisation. My answer is always the same: 'I have no idea if these strategies are "enough". What is clear is that no one has "*the* solution", or else our problems would be solved. If you are able to let go of the belief that there must be a way out because the problem is so big, then you are free to actually take the action you can in the settings in which you find yourself.'[157]

I don't mean to underestimate how difficult it is to take the lessons just discussed to heart. Our individual lives are the greatest finite hurdle we face, because one of life's dominant impulses is to maintain itself. Every person is born with instincts geared towards growth as an individual entity. These prompt us to learn and find our gifts. However, if these instincts also lead us to clutch hold of our lives as if death is a preventable failure, then each game that helped us win before is projected into the future, in an effort to suspend time by playing the game over and over again. This results in defending the status quo and prevents us from being able to stand back from what is, and assess whether it is time to let go. And so, inadvertently, we restrain and perhaps strangle the future.

Grasping at life in this way does not just prevent us from letting other people have their time in the sun. Even *within* our individual lives, it may prevent us from recognising when it is time to give up on the particular game we are now playing. There is such liberation in letting go, even if you did not make the mark you hoped. Surely everyone is familiar with the relief of failure. When I don't get a research grant for example, I can almost feel the molecules of some heavy substance vanish from my body leaving me as light as air. Now, praise be, I can start again with the flood of ideas that had to be silenced while this other game was still in play.

Finite play extends the anxious hope that our personal lives will continue as before into our social structures. These become like one's individual being – entities that must be preserved. Just as we resist entertaining the possibility of death because it may seem like an invitation, we similarly resist entertaining the possibility that our social structures will one day collapse. The very thought reveals a void that can surely be avoided if we just, well, *don't* think about it. An illustration of this mind-set can be seen in our habit of mathematical projection. A quick search of the Internet informs me that, by 2050, the world's population will be 9.7 billion, China's economy will be the largest (followed by the USA), and life expectancy in Japan will be 91.58 years.[158] Such projections imagine a future which is not a future, but a continuation of the past. They make invisible the likelihood of radical discontinuities that occur without warning within any complex system. They suggest that the way to play is as we have always done.

—◦—◦—◦—

As people concerned for the common good, we too often yearn for the past. I hear frequent talk of how things 'used to be better'. Most commonly this is before neo-liberalism, but it may also be before the green revolution in agriculture, or the industrial revolution, or even before people became farmers. I do it too. I swear the young women of today are less feminist than in my day and that universities have become more technocratic. But I think our deeper collective wisdom is that what we have now is a hybrid of 'better' and 'worse' and that, anyway, we can't go back. Time sweeps up all the bits and pieces it encounters and weaves them into a unique pattern in which nothing can be left behind.

By yearning for the past and focusing on what is 'worse than before', we leave the future gaping. Yes, to try and pin it down is a problematic play. But a little visioning does not go astray. People need to see what could be, or it is terribly hard to give up on what is. We need something vivid and tangible to shake the dominant narrative that business as usual will bring a materialist utopia and increasingly long lives. We also need something light and open so as not to tie the hands of those who come after us, insisting that they must carry our dream forward. As infinite players, it is surely our task to hand the game on, rather than set it in stone. To do this we must offer possibilities for the future and strive to let go when the time is right.

15. Changing the rules versus maintaining the rules

> The rules of the infinite game must change over
> time or the game will cease; To change or break
> the rules of a finite game is a violation

And now, with game feature 15, we come to the conclusion of Part One. Infinite players and a society that embraced infinite play would not be scared of the endings and beginnings that time brings. Life = Time = Change. To resist change is to resist time is to resist life. Such players would be aiming to open spaces for life to flourish now and into an unpredictable future. Infinite players know that today's rules – that is, the various finite games we have constructed for ourselves – are only management tools, and well short of the best we can do. They also know that to mistake the current management tools for a permanent solution to living well together is fatal to our collective future.

Some societies *have* made fatal mistakes. Jared Diamond's book *Collapse* is full of examples of these.[159] One of the most famous is Easter Island, a small island in the Pacific that appears to have become completely deforested by its human inhabitants sometime between AD 900 and 1722. Trees were used for building, cultural artefacts, fuel and human cremation, as well as being cleared for agriculture. Eventually, however, the forest was gone. When all of Easter Island's tree species became extinct so did its land birds, depriving people of sources of wild food as well as the resources needed for building. Ultimately, the society collapsed. From our current lens, it would seem as if the Easter Islanders failed to adjust their finite games in response to the changing environment.

From an outsider's perspective, it seems almost beyond belief that a society could persist with finite games that are destroying its very foundation for life. But when you understand how finite games operate, it seems only too possible. If we are not careful – and by that I mean, if we do not have a process for standing back from and assessing our games – the game at hand becomes the thing. Finite games lure us into doing what it takes to win. They encourage tunnel vision and disregard for the big picture. The rules are set pieces that we attempt to use to our advantage. If we attempt to stray from the rules, the other players push us back in line: to change or break the rules is a violation. Finite players may even be aware that the game is creating dangerous ripples that put life in jeopardy, but this does not mean they know how to extract themselves from it. Think of the millions who know that our method and rate of consumption is unsustainable and yet who continue to consume. The game of consumption is so endemic it is extraordinarily hard not to go along.

————

This exploration of finite and infinite plays in Western society and what it might mean to give more attention to the values of the infinite game – as communities and advocates for the common good – is just a starting point. If the symbol has captured your imagination, then you will have recognised the infinite game and finite games in other settings. And you have probably disagreed with some of my arguments or examples. I hope, like me, you have found these games useful for seeing how power gets stuck in particular people and institutions, including those initially created to disrupt power. Finite games have a gravitational pull maintained by their demand for focus and appeal to self-preservation. They are like spinning tops: once they have survived the first wobbles, they need little extra force to maintain them – at least until a final catastrophe knocks them down.

I now see finite games in every branch or franchise of a larger entity, in every competition, in every old boys' network, in every meeting in which I am confused as to what is really going on, and in every claim to ownership. None of these shibboleths are sacred, and I refuse to bow down and worship the winners. What is (closer to) sacred are our deepest values and attempting to keep these alive inside ourselves and in our social interactions, now and into the future. I suspect that my efforts to contribute to a better world have always been about keeping these values alive. And when I engage with others who sense something better is possible, it seems to me that they are trying to do the same.

The infinite game is one way of talking about the commonality and wisdom that underpins our diverse approaches. The finite/infinite tension is always present. It is inside our psyches, our families, our neighbourhoods, our workplaces and our cultural milieus. The most we can do is try and nurture infinite play in each of these places and regularly reflect on whether our finite games are serving us well. That is pretty much it, really. Oh, and we must not forget to bask in the spontaneous warmth and creativity of everyday people and our crazy, perhaps doomed, but irresistible struggle to become better, as individuals and a collective. As Elizabeth Gilbert writes in her magnificent autobiography *Eat, Pray, Love: One Woman's Search for Everything*:[160]

> The devout of this world perform their rituals without guarantee that anything good will ever come of it. We all agree that it would be easier to sleep in, and many of us do, but for millennia there have been others who choose instead to get up before the sun and wash their faces and go to their prayers. And then fiercely try to hold on to their devotional convictions throughout the lunacy of another day.

This is what being an infinite player or a community that cares about our lives together means. Getting up each day, remembering what matters, and trying like hell to live that in the confusion of real life. It does not mean knowing what is right. Sometimes it might just mean rejecting that which is clearly wrong (as far as you can tell). And, I humbly suggest, this process may be aided by imagining life as an infinite game. Not because it is, exactly, but because imagining it so might help to focus us on what truly matters.

Part Two

The
Infinite
Player

When someone I know is about to have her first baby, I always give the same advice: 'This will probably hurt more than you can imagine is possible for a normal event. When you think to yourself that it must be going wrong because of the depth of the pain or because it is blatantly obvious that to push will tear you in half, try to keep with it. You don't need to be confident, you just need to be persistent.' The woman looks at me with an indulgent half-smile that means she will make up her own mind thank you, but I know I am right.

So imagine my delight when I came across Alistair McIntosh, an ex-university academic and Scottish activist, saying something similar in relation to challenging the status quo:[161]

> We fear the whole process getting out of hand. Can we handle it? Where might it all end? Won't people think we're peculiar, and then there'll be no way back on to strait-street? We also fear that if we engage the Powers it might be for the wrong motives. It may just be ego; indeed, we know ourselves, and so we realise that to some extent it *will* be ego! Also, it may be that the corporation, or the Government, or 'the system', or whatever it is represents an unresolved complex with a parent or some other authority figure from childhood. There's nothing really wrong with the world – we're just projecting our own crap out on to it! . . . At the one extreme, then, we think we're not good enough to testify for a better world. At the other, we fear going crazy, screwing up, failing, being crucified or ego-tripping our way to the madhouse.

In other words, if you are attempting radical change (or even a tiny change that challenges 'how we do things around here'), there's a good chance that there will be times when it will feel worse than it possibly could if you were really doing the right thing. The revolution, we must remember, will not be funded. More than that, it will be resisted both inside and outside ourselves. Giving birth is actually much easier. It's all over in a couple of days at the very most, and everyone wants that baby out. Not everyone wants the revolution. So the second part of this book is an attempt to speak to all ego-tripping activists or anyone else who cares about the common good, and provide an infinite game perspective on how to feel the fear, doubt and disorientation, and play anyway.

It has five chapters that each concern a principle that the (want to be) infinite player is invited to bear in mind. These don't involve restating the features of the game itself, as I am assuming you have attended to and responded to these as you wish. They are instead the core challenges and strategies that I suggest make us better individual players. I also want to make it clear that I am not trying to claim I am a particularly good player myself. My credentials in writing this guidance are more about my intense interest in becoming better, and my years of observing, talking with and researching those whose actions and outlook I admire. The five principles are: *hold finite games lightly*, *seek and express authenticity*, *strive for radical cooperation*, *beware the trickster* and always *reflect and learn*.

—◦—◦—◦—

Chapter Six

Hold Finite Games Lightly

The starting point for holding finite games lightly is to realise that you are a player. You have choices – and so does everyone else. Good players play hard and act as if the game matters. As we are talking about life, this means *feeling* your life. It means allowing the joys and sorrows life brings to wash through you like rogue waves, and inform (but not determine) your decisions. But equally it means knowing that you are not of much consequence in the scheme of things. Like all games, your life will end, probably leaving just a faint trace that will soon pass.

In addition, if you think of life as a game, or series of games, then you know that it exists in the action between players. A game of tennis is not a game of tennis until two people play with each other. And if they know exactly how it will turn out that day, then it isn't much of a game. It might be a pleasant way to get some exercise, but it will not be truly open in the way of games that grab our full attention. Similarly, you cannot control what happens to you – or what will happen to the world – as a result of the actions you take. There is no protection from connectedness.

Accepting that you are a player, no more and no less, echoes the wisdom of the Rabbi Simcha Bunim of Peschischa. Rabbi Bunim stated that we should all carry two slips of paper, one in our right pocket and one in our left. On one is written, 'For my sake the world was created', and on the other, 'I am but dust and ashes'. Liberation comes when you simultaneously realise you have just as much right as anyone else to express your inner truths, and that whether or not you claim this right does not matter much. Liberation is the starting point for play. Who ever heard of playing when you are in chains?

———o———o———o———

So how do we play the finite games we are immersed in with all the passion needed to play well and still hold them lightly? I am going to make four suggestions: we move between *being a player and being an observer*; we learn to *live uncomfortably with hypocrisy*; we *set up mini-games to help us manage our choices*; and we *act without expectation of results*.

Before getting into these suggestions, it is important to note that infinite players play at least three types of finite games. One type is the games we play to try and promote the common good. These are the games we explicitly recognise as attempts to forward infinite values. They might include, for example, being a volunteer for an NGO, participating in a community garden, becoming vegan, being the union representative at our workplace, or standing for elected office. Another is the games we play to survive within the society in which we exist. This might include owning a home, having a job, or using a car to get around town. Finally, we may also have games in which we are trying to win for the sake of winning. Examples of such games might be attempting to be promoted at work, investing in the housing market with the hope of making enough money to retire young, or aiming to have our (eco, fair-trade!) product in every supermarket in the country.

Strictly speaking, the second and especially third types of game are the domains of finite players, but those of us who want to be better infinite players are still whole human beings. That means acknowledging from the start, that you (and me) will almost certainly be keeping all these types of finite games in play. Besides which, one action may involve more than one of these games. So, here I am, acting for the common good by writing this book. But it is also my job to write. Therefore, it is in part a survival game. And I can't deny my desire to win for the sake of winning. If people read it and are inspired, this will stoke my ego. As Alistair McIntosh said in the quotation given earlier, our motivations tend to be mixed, which translates to games that are rarely exactly one type or another. So, as we go through this chapter, I will be ducking between these different types of games, offering possibilities for holding the whole lot lightly.

Move between being a player and being an observer

In his 1994 book *Breakfast at the Victory: The Mysticism of Ordinary Experience*, James P. Carse wrote: 'At the heart of all our passions – grief, joy, alarm, lust – resides a clear-eyed witness ever awake and innocent, untouched by these storms.'[162] Here, Carse captures the difference between being a player and being an observer. A player, as I am using it, is someone who throws themselves into a game – with the entailing grief, joy, alarm and lust. An observer, on the other hand, is a clear-eyed witness, who knows at some level that it is just a game. To be only an observer of life – that is, to actually attain the detachment that is promoted by some traditions – is not to *live*. James Hillman, a psychoanalyst, has forcefully described the dangers of seeking detachment – which he calls transcendence – thus:[163]

> I think it's an absolute horror that someone could . . . think that his personal, little, tiny self-transcendence is more important than the world and the beauty of the world: the trees, the animals, the people, the buildings, the culture. What is the psychological pull of this transcendence? What is happening in the psyche that could make a person so incredibly self-centered? So self-centered to say, 'Good-bye brothers, good-bye children, good-bye wife, good-bye flowers, good-bye everything. I'm off to the snowy heights. I want an imageless white liberation and freedom from the cycle of birth and rebirth.' And what in the world is going on in the psyche that this delusional system can so take hold? I think one [that] has fallen to the archetype of the spirit.

The point Hillman is making, I think, is that there is something profoundly disturbing about wanting to completely disentangle ourselves from the stuff of life. In the language of our games, it is to seek a finite game that cradles us by attempting to deny our porous, antifragile natures. An understandable move, given life's ability to slam into us and leave us winded, but not an infinite game move. Having said that, if we are *only* players, we risk being suffocated by our games, unable to leave them or change them. We need some ability to float above ourselves and take a look at what we have got ourselves into.

In the finite games that we are playing to win for the sake of winning, we would do well to cultivate the observer in us. Winning such finite games is, by definition, to support the competitive ethos that produces a winner. So you made a million dollars by investing in a wind-turbine company at the right time? That may well show foresight, business acumen, faith in alternative energy, patience and courage. *Genuine* congratulations from me, these are qualities I lack in relation to investment. (I told you I am hopeless at, and so won't play, Monopoly – so imagine how I feel about a game of Monopoly where the winner gets to keep all their stuff!) However, by making a million dollars, you have also now pulled more than your share of wealth out of the commons. That is a price you must pay – no matter how worthy your motives. To start to feel you are entitled to that money, or as if you are to be taken more seriously as a human being because of your victory, is a very finite play.

To use another example: I always cringe at some level when I am introduced as an associate professor from the University of Auckland. I know that sounds impressive in many of the circles I move in, and it did take work and some worthy qualities on my part to get to where I am. But, at another level, I am fully aware that I am no better than those further down the system (or worse than those higher up, for that matter). More than that, to get to my position I had to compromise on some qualities I value – like the amount of time and consideration I have given to my teaching and students over the years. The gaps I have left have no doubt caused people to suffer and struggle more than necessary, or been filled by colleagues – potentially colleagues who have done less well within the system than me.

We could all do with nurturing our imposter syndrome. Pauline Clance and Rose Imes, psychologists from Georgia State University, coined the concept of the 'imposter phenomenon' to describe the sense of not being worthy of a particular role. It was first used to refer to women in high-status positions who believed an error had been made in appointing them and that they would be found out. To quote from Clance and Imes's 1978 article: 'One woman professor said, "I'm not good enough to be on the faculty here. Some mistake was made in the selection process." Another, the chairperson of her department, said, "Obviously I'm in this position because my abilities have been over-estimated."'[164] (Don't you love the modesty of these women? Those were the days.) These days the imposter syndrome is used more broadly to describe how many of us feel on acquiring a new identity, that we are not the real thing. We are not a real married person, chief executive, or bank teller. We are *just pretending*. The conclusion we are encouraged to draw in most references to the imposter syndrome is that we *are* the real thing – look, your name is on the door! But an alternative perspective is – yes, sister, you, like everyone else, are an imposter.[165] Never take your winning role for granted. It is not a right that you need not question.

—o—o—o—

In the games we are playing to forward the common good, taking them seriously is surely part of the play. If our game is attempting to keep what we most value in play, then it would be tragic to shake it off as if it is merely a million dollars or an academic title. It will, and should, hurt when we lose the fight to stop another McDonald's being built in our neighbourhood or when our government takes no serious steps to reduce greenhouse gas emissions despite the plethora of evidence and logic that we have helped put before them. If it did not hurt, then we have become numb to the issues at stake, which means we don't really care; and if we don't really care, then why bother? Drinking margaritas beside the pool is a much easier way to pass the time.

At the same time, however, we must not get lost in the particulars of our common-good game to the detriment of the values on which it is based. I currently have a role as the coordinator of a sustainability network within the science faculty at my university. When a student comes to me with an idea (compost bins in the student commons, improved bike stands, banning the sale of bottled water, providing dishwashing facilities), I have to prevent myself from saying, 'Yes, but . . . it's been tried before/it's far more complicated than you think – how about you forward this or that goal of our network instead.' I am so caught up in our network's struggles to effect change, I am sometimes tempted to forget that our network's goals aren't the point. The point is to build a sustainability culture that welomes all players. I know from my own experience how disorienting it is to be put in your place by people who you thought would welcome your suggestion. It is as if a precious offering has been kicked aside, leaving you feeling inappropriate, naïve, and even ugly.

A more infinite play, and the response I manage to give enthusiastic students when I am on the ball, is to listen carefully, offer support, and most of all to show as thoroughly as possible that their energy is *absolutely appropriate*. Yes, we must care about the particulars of our common-good game, but not to the extent that the bigger picture fades from view.

Live, uncomfortably, with hypocrisy

Learning to see beyond the particulars of your common-good game is one thing. A more difficult dilemma concerns the tension that everyone who has a vision for a better world faces between 'being the change' and pushing for change through current communication and political channels. Hypocrisy – the feeling that we are advocating for something we are contradicting in our actions – is a constant companion for most of us.

Hypocrisy is fairly inevitable, because the trouble with 'being the change' is that, taken to an extreme, it means not participating in social life. Not participating in social life means rejecting the most obvious means of rallying support and challenging the status quo. In interviews that my student Daniel Farrant did with environmental activists, one said, 'I don't think what the world needs right now is yet another group of people fucking off into the hills and creating a model of what most people can't have.'[166] In other words, there is such a big distance between where we are now and how the world might be, that to live the dream – whatever your version of the dream is – is also to ignore the need to bridge that gap. As William James wrote after studying the lives of saints and noticing how isolated many became in seeking to live without sin: 'Purity . . . is not the one thing needful; and it is better that a life should contract many a dirt-mark, than forfeit usefulness in its efforts to remain unspotted.'[167] (I don't mean to imply that there is no place for modelling an alternative lifestyle, but rather that this is certainly not the only way to keep the infinite game in play.)

Still, to simply ignore the challenge to be the change is equally extreme. It would be to step away from the infinite game principle that says the game is always being played in the present. The dream – in its pure form – is a perpetual illusion. So we must learn to live *now* in a massively imperfect world, that sometimes requires damaging what we know to be precious. But as part of living the only life we have, we must surely bear witness to what we value, even if it seems to make no difference to the world at large. In the following passage, the philosopher Roger Gottlieb puts this clearly in relation to religious environmentalism. While he uses the terms 'religious' and 'spiritual', these could be substituted with suitable equivalents that capture the underlying ethos of the infinite game. Similarly, it is possible to replace 'environmentalism' with any form of orientation towards the common good.[168]

Environmentalism offers a series of choices about daily behaviour that encompass the smallest details with an exacting discipline . . . [M]ost environmentalists know that the real ballgame is institutional, legal, and deeply economic – not personal . . . Yet the point is that the religious quality of everyday environmental actions is not measured solely by its immediate effects. It stems, rather, from a characteristically spiritual sense that everything we do has moral meaning. Regardless of how much any given act helps to conserve resources or heal the earth, it must be done anyway, for 'this is the kind of person I wish to be' and 'it just is the right thing to do' . . . For any serious religious dedication includes a lifelong attempt to mould the self in accordance with the deepest truths of the universe. Religious action may be aimed at a larger goal – repair of the world, sustaining the community of believers – but it also shapes personal conduct . . . the ardent environmentalist has parameters of behavior that require self-discipline and self-knowledge as well as public duties.

Charles Eisenstein, the author of *Sacred Economics*, goes even further than Gottlieb, arguing that there may be force-fields that allow our small actions to resonate through the world.[169] This means that when we act for justice – perhaps, for example, by bringing the contribution of a colleague to the attention of our boss – this action is felt more widely than just between the people involved. Similarly, when we bake bread from local flour, or compost, or refuse to buy clothes made in low-wage conditions, our efforts may be amplified in ways we don't yet understand. Whether or not such force-fields exist in the way Eisenstein is suggesting, they are a useful construct for articulating our sense that our everyday actions are somehow a crucial part of what it means to advocate for change or to be an infinite player. It is also certainly true that our personal practices don't go unnoticed. I trust people who try to walk the talk. I listen to them more closely as I assume they are not just trying to manipulate me as a pawn in a hidden game.

––◇––◇––◇––

Where does this leave us? Should you fly to promote the dangers of climate change or only engage in Skype exchanges that may have less impact on those who are listening? Should you wear a fair-trade T-shirt rather than a tidy mass-produced suit when presenting to corporates on the benefits of introducing a living wage? Should you spend your time growing your own vegetables or instead lobby the city council to provide garden allotments to urban families? There are, of course, no absolute answers to any of these questions, but part of holding our finite games lightly is to recognise these tensions and negotiate them as best we can. Whatever we decide – to do the Skype call or jump on the plane – we should live with our decision uncomfortably. This acknowledges players who choose differently from us, and leaves us open to better solutions to what is an unsolvable problem.

Living, uncomfortably, with hypocrisy also acknowledges, as the social movement researchers Max Haiven and Alex Khasnabish have pointed out, that our privilege may not allow us to be truly revolutionary.[170] If you are middle-class, and drive your daughter to dance lessons (me), or live in a gentrified suburb (me), or have a stable job that gives you status (me), or have access to reliable modern health care (me), then unless you give it all up, you are, in your own way, helping reify privilege. Given that you are almost certainly not going to give it *all* up, it may be better to acknowledge the contradiction implicit in middle-class life than to attempt to justify your privilege, or to feel it prevents you from speaking against that which you benefit from. You can call for increased taxes for high-income earners without donating the additional money you get while these taxes are low. At the same time, your message would be more powerful if you did not keep this money. You, we, need to live with this limit to our revolutionary potential, but never quite accept its inevitability.

You may also want to think through how to face the accusation, or implication, that you are a hypocrite. I once gave a verbal submission on improving bike lanes to Auckland's city council, and was asked by a councillor if I owned a car. I had no idea how to reply, as I do own a car but felt if I admitted that it would refute the integrity of my message. I wanted to say something like, 'Your point being?' when I knew exactly what his point was. As it happened, he was instantly hushed by several other councillors so I was saved from my awkwardness.

It is, quite frankly, horrible to feel that our personal integrity is being challenged. So next time someone asks if I own a car when I am suggesting we rearrange our transport networks to make less room for cars and more room for bikes, I am going to say: 'Yes, I own a car. I think very hard before I use my car, and when I do use it, it is always with some regret. I wish I lived in a city where I was not torn in this way, and where I could go about my daily life by bike and train or bus more easily. Meanwhile, like you, I want to fully participate in the life of the city, including in the opportunity you are offering me to explain my personal practices and compromises. And so while I ride my bike a lot, even in the rain and the dark and even when I am tired, sometimes I drive my car.' Well, I may not say exactly that, as it could come across as a bit pompous depending on the situation, but neither am I going to slump in my chair and act as if I have been caught out.

Set up mini-games to manage your choices

One way to hold our finite games lightly and navigate the tension between being the change and living within the system we have inherited, is to set up mini-games that give us boundaries and direction. One of my favourite examples is the rubbish-free project of Matthew Luxon and Waveney Warth, whose household generates almost no waste to landfill.[171] They began their project when living in Christchurch, and have various rules – rules that suit them as a couple, but that they also take seriously. For example, one rule is that the only waste that counts is that which comes from their home. So theoretically they could buy coffee in a disposable cup when they are out and about (although they don't). They are also allowed to use products whose containers can be recycled through the local council or another provider.

I also greatly admire the policy of those at the Public Interest Research Centre in the UK to travel overland rather than fly to events in Europe. These mini-games provide the participants with certainty about how to respond to hypocrisy-related challenges in at least one arena. They are also powerful communication tools in themselves. They invite others to consider how to adjust their own lives or organisations in keeping with what they value most deeply.

One of my mini-games at the moment – I have been doing it for about four years – is to cook vegan dinners (very occasionally I use eggs that are SPCA-approved or better, or a small amount of dairy milk, and I abandon the rules when we are camping). I set up these self-imposed rules because I did not want to refuse other people's food. There are numerous reasons why I dislike refusing food, including my experience that it is easier to relate to people if you eat, and are seen to enjoy, what you are offered. I also cannot quite shake the notion – even though I know plenty of readers will want to challenge me on this – that some animal products are part of a balanced diet. This means I don't want to 'be' vegan, despite being concerned about animal welfare and the environmental implications of how we produce meat and dairy products. Then one day it occurred to me that food prohibitions don't have to be about what you eat, they can equally as easily be about what you serve others. The fact that we encourage food identities based on the former is not written in stone; in fact, it can be rather easily seen as a product of our individualism. So being a vegan cook is a little game I have invented to find a way through some of the ethics of food.

The icing on the cake of these sorts of games – the ones we set up for ourselves to reduce the constant need to think about our choices in a particular domain – is that we never lose awareness that they are just games. Johan Huizinga has discussed how cultural rituals begin as play, in which the players know there is an illusion at their heart.[172] The rain dancers, for example, don't actually believe their dancing will make the rains arrive; Jesus's disciples did not experience the wine they drank becoming blood. Over time, however, these rituals become mistaken for The Truth – perhaps never by the elders or priests who arrange them – but by the culture at large. And once rituals are holders of The Truth, we are caught in the finite game's idolatry trap, which makes it so hard to respond to new truths. But if it is just your own little game, well, you know it is a bit of a lark. You never really believe it is the answer to life, and so you can also let it go and move on when the time comes.

Act without expectation of results

The final piece to holding finite games lightly is to act without expectation of results. As with so much that springs from imagining life as an infinite game, this is an ancient wisdom that can be found in many theologies and philosophies.[173] It applies particularly strongly to social-change advocates because, as Max Haiven and Alex Khasnabish have claimed, attempting to challenge the status quo also means learning to dwell 'on the cusp of failure'.[174] Actually, let's say it more directly than that – challenging the status quo means *being awash in almost constant failure*. Not only is there the big failure of seeing minimal large-scale change, there are also the multiple small failures that occur when particular plans go awry. In interviews that Sonja Tepavac, Pat Bullen and I did with eight long-term political activists, many spoke of a sense of failure that extended over long periods of time. One said: '. . . the 80s and 90s were really hard, trade unions were smashed in a lot of cases, people just fought and fought and fought unsuccessfully against the changes and I think people just got exhausted, tried really hard, didn't succeed very often.'[175]

Somehow we need to learn to live with the realisation that if we look at what we have achieved too closely, we may come up with – nothing. Nothing? After all those tedious meetings when I could have been drinking margaritas by the pool?

We can, I suggest, overcome this demoralising conclusion by trying our best to live without expectation of results. In the infinite game, there is no finish line or limit to the breadth and depth of the playing field. To take a simple example, I am currently part of a group that is attempting to persuade our university to sell its investments in companies that produce fossil fuels. We are part of the divestment movement initiated by 350.org that has gained considerable momentum at the time of writing. Just to be clear, the divestment goal is the *very reason* our group exists. It would be silly to give up at the first hurdle. On the other hand, we don't need to judge the validity of our actions by whether our university takes the hoped-for action, despite this being our raison d'être. We have already created a partnership between students and staff and raised questions about the ethics of the university's investments. These are surely good outcomes, whatever happens next. At the moment, it doesn't look likely we will achieve our goal anytime soon.

On a much grander scale, a New Zealand anti-apartheid protest movement in 1981 aimed to stop a national tour of the South African rugby team. The tour went ahead but the protest movement was enormously important in igniting national debates about racism and justice. Gandhi is associated with non-violence, and yet the independence of India, one of his aims, resulted in considerable violence as India and Pakistan were partitioned. Jesus, María Elena Moyano, Martin Luther King, Steve Biko, and untold others have been killed for their attempts at social change.

So the results of our actions depend to a large extent on where you draw the finish line and how far you extend the net – and these artificial boundaries are meant to help us, not make us despair. As players, it is our absolute right to shift the goal posts as often as necessary in order to help us understand how our actions (may) have rippled through the world around us. If it still seems we have taken one step forward and two steps back, then we need to remember that the really important issue is whether we acted in good faith. That, after all, is the best we can do – and even that is a pretty tall order.

—◦—◦—◦—

If we let go of the need to ring-fence an outcome and say, 'I did that', then we may also be more willing to take action which has no measurable outcome or whose outcome cannot be attributed to us.[176] I give a lot of talks and workshops, and generally have little idea of the influence these have. It is lovely when people give me positive feedback, but overall the impact of my talks is something of a mystery to me. I sense that what I am doing is useful, but I cannot (or do not) measure exactly how. In most circumstances, I feel that to do a formal evaluation would be to suggest I was after an exchange – I give you inspiration; you give me feedback that I can use in my performance review. That is not the spirit in which I want to operate.

If you take action whose outcome can't be attributed to you, you become a faery. Faeries are elusive creatures that fly in when no one is looking, do their mischief, and then disappear.[177] They add a little spice to the infinite game. A friend of mine told me how she altered the minutes of a meeting without anyone noticing to expose a misuse of organisational resources. Graffiti artists are also faeries. So are those who put subversive stickers on particularly finite game-driven products at supermarkets. I would like to put stickers on all the bottled water at our local supermarket saying: 'Tap water is better than me.' Although, having declared that desire in this book, it would now not be very faery-like. We don't always have to stand up for what we do. If your action is intended to be subversive, perhaps a subversive medium increases its poetry and impact.

—○—○—○—

To conclude, holding finite games lightly means being able to rise above them from time to time, and recognise that there is always something more important at stake than the game at hand. We are currently trained to devote considerable time and attention towards coming out on top. The ideal citizen studies towards her career on leaving school with retirement planning commencing with her first job. If her career and investments do not turn out as planned, she goes down with them. This creates an inhumane burden to calculate the impact of today's decisions on an impossibly complex future. Similarly, if we see our finite games designed to forward infinite values as vitally important for life itself, we also become trapped in a need to win. That very act of clutching is in itself a move outside the infinite game. I suspect you can feel it when it happens – I certainly can. It has the texture of fear and greed; it creates impatience towards others and unwillingness to listen. We can justify what we are doing for sure, but at some level we also feel the shame that people do when they pretend to know The Truth or to be entitled to what they have acquired.

It is especially important to hold our career, investments, and all our other personal getting-ahead games with as little concern as possible for how they turn out. That allows us not to be held back from doing what we feel is right for the world by our desire to win according to the terms set by the status quo. If you are made redundant or buy a house at the peak of the market, all that will happen is that you will join the history of good men and women before you who also lost at these games. Is that so terribly bad? If you do not win, perhaps it was bad luck, or perhaps it was an inability to narrow your focus and deny your emotions in the way often required in these endeavours. I don't want to disavow the anger and self-pity engendered by losing at the games that we are told are the markers of success in our society. I still feel horrendous waves of self-pity and regret from time to time about my own losses. But the infinite player in us knows that these games are the least meaningful part of our lives. Our values-based action means so much more.

So live, care, be attached. The world was made for you. But simultaneously step into the role of a clear-eyed witness from time to time, and remember that you are a mere drop in a turbulent ocean.

Chapter Seven

Seek and Express Authenticity

You have to be a bit uncool to try and be authentic. Scholars know there is no such thing as a 'real self', as who we are is always slippery and hard to define, as well as being deeply influenced by our culture and experiences. The powers that be in politics and business often argue that authenticity (if it comes into the picture at all) must be sacrificed for strategy when the going gets tough. Even social movements frequently stress *collective* action, which is sometimes assumed to be a greater good than *authentic* action.

Authenticity can be summed up from these perspectives as ignorant, pointless, or distracting. It sounds dangerously like new-age gospel or yet another way of encouraging people to put themselves first and foremost. But from the perspective of an infinite player, authenticity is vital. Infinite players are not particularly concerned with whether or not there is a 'real self'. They know that we are playing games and need not, indeed cannot, establish rock-solid certainty in order to begin. Infinite players are just after devices that help us live well together. Authenticity, I suggest, is one such device.

—o—o—o—

The essence of authenticity is trusting to an intuitive, feeling process of decision-making.[178] It is, as Andy Fisher the ecopsychologist puts it, the opposite of 'going through life on the basis of stuck patterns, old ideas, introjected beliefs, habitual reactions, other people's opinions, superego warnings, expert advice, and archaic fantasies'.[179] It is often the dominant mode by which we play the games we know as games, like soccer, Settlers of Catan, Cluedo, and table tennis. When we are playing these games, we have to take action – sometimes quickly or even automatically – and much of the fun is in trusting ourselves. There is nothing more tedious than having someone advise your every move. Even if you win under these conditions, what exactly have you won? The person-best-able-to-follow-advice award?

Authenticity isn't easy, however, and nor is it static. If we want to trust ourselves, we need to understand ourselves. We need to know what we love to do. We also need to recognise when we are acting out of spite and other motives that maintain old games which are not helping anyone. Much of this is about identifying the trickster, as will be discussed in Chapter Nine.

We also need to become intimate with the domain we are working within. You cannot play intuitive soccer without knowing the rules. Similarly, you cannot forward the project of living well together without some understanding of how social life works. As James P. Carse described in a book of essays published ten years after *Finite and Infinite Games*, great poetry comes from learning the techniques of your art form and then abandoning both 'ego' and technique 'at just the right moment, allowing the poetic to enter on its own terms'.[180]

Authenticity, then, is not exactly about expressing *yourself*; it is more about allowing your sense of what needs to be done to be the final decider. At times that may include knowing that you do not know enough and seeking more information. Authentic practice raises questions such as: 'Can I really follow the logic behind this proposal, or am I just tempted to agree out of conformity or confusion?' 'Is acting in this way consistent with the kind of person I want to be, even if I would rather do something else right now?' 'Is this the time to make a fuss, even if I cannot articulate myself clearly using the rules of the game at hand?'

—o—o—o—

One of the hardest aspects of seeking authenticity is knowing when to keep probing and when to back off, even though you sense something is amiss. Recently, for example, someone in a climate-change group I belong to suggested proposing the government set up a future-oriented think tank of young people who would get their student loans written off in exchange for participation. I responded by saying the think tank was a great idea, but that if participants had their student loans excused this would immediately create a sense of unfairness in the group. There would either be considerable variability in the size of their loans, or those without large loans would not be attracted to participate. Either way, the financial status of the participants would be in play, and that did not seem right to me. Another group member immediately refuted my position. I then had the choice: push my position, support the proposal, or back off. I chose to back off. Alistair McIntosh and Matt Carmichael have called backing off in such situations to 'withhold your blessing'.[181] Of course, always backing off would be to never take a stand, and so to give up your right to play. But sometimes withholding your blessing allows you to acknowledge that you don't have the capacity to figure this one out right now. It is a little like the 'not proven' verdict available to Scottish courts.

In the case above, withholding my blessing was a minor act that avoided deep thought. Withholding your blessing, however, can be a radical political move. Imagine if people only took jobs which they saw as genuinely useful. Under those conditions, I suspect whole industries would disappear.[182] How many people can actually see the benefit of developing a more effective shampoo for brittle hair? Or designing advertisements for instant finance companies? Or working in an armaments factory? Or being a lobbyist for the tobacco industry? As infinite players, I think it is vital we nurture our courage to stay away from that for which we have no vision; because the more people who do that, the more the status quo is tested. If it was just lack of imagination on your part that kept you from the shampoo industry when you graduated with a degree in chemistry, then others will fill that gap. But if such work is, in the end, not of great value, then authentic action will reveal it as such.

––o––o––o––

The struggle for authenticity also brings people together.[183] If you think about it, people feel united when we tap the same felt experience (or sense that we are). This is why humour, particularly black humour, is so uplifting – it gives us a moment of recognition in regard to a situation that is dangerously out of our control. You may have seen the series of YouTube videos that came out after Donald Trump was elected which featured countries acknowledging that America is first, but could they please be second?[184] I have also come across intriguing suggestions that leadership is about embodying and articulating 'the direction or yearnings of the group' or 'the uncertainties or anxieties of [the] era'.[185] The most influential, in other words, are those who dare to name or practise what the rest of us feel to be true but have not quite got our heads around. When people are simply going through the motions of life, there is no point of connection with others. Connection only comes when we go deeper.

If we work to articulate what people feel in relation to the status quo, we can potentially create unity amongst those who are ready to listen. The feminism of the 1970s named the tedium of being trapped in a suburban nuclear household. Around the same time, anti-apartheid activists named the injustice (and absurdity) of trying to separate people on the basis of colour. These truths were easy to feel, and so helped underpin movements. Social analysis without any emotional depth is a finite move. Social analysis that bounces off emotional depth is an infinite move.

—o—o—o—

Finally, being authentic is all part of keeping freedom and creativity and all those other human joys alive. Being inauthentic is deadly, deadly dull. It is like a one-person logjam that prevents life from flowing freely.[186] You do not have to be sure of yourself or refuse to compromise – you just need to keep tinkering with how you are in the world, and withhold your blessing when what is put before you does not seem right. Because when you do act from some deep yearning, it is like slicing the status quo open, jumping through and yelling, 'Who wants to come too?'

Chapter Eight

Strive for Radical Cooperation

Several years ago, early on a Sunday morning when I was on the back deck of our house, I experienced a profound shift in perspective. I love the early morning and at the weekend I am often up two hours before anyone else in our household. My favourite activity is to go outside and read, accompanied by as many cups of coffee as needed to fill the time available. I read slowly, as I prefer challenging material at that time of day, looking up and thinking for at least as much time as I look at the printed words. This particular Sunday came after a week of small work failures – an article rejected, not winning an award I had been nominated for, a collective grant application not making it through the first round. As is often the case, while those failures were hurtful, they also brought moments of warmth – hysterical laugher in the corridor with a colleague over our run of rejections, a lovely email exchange between those of us who were on the grant application, and huge gratitude for my family who largely think articles, awards and grants are 'boring work stuff'.

Anyway, so there I was – one cup of coffee in, luxuriating in the hiatus of that weekend morning when the events of the previous week were at a distance. Suddenly, while gazing over the garden, I felt, overwhelmingly, inarticulately, how fundamental cooperation is to life. I looked intensely at the small pōhutukawa tree growing off the corner of the deck and saw how its leaves were oriented towards the sun and appeared to suck in the light, capturing it for life on Earth. The thicker branches were home to patches of lichen, and I saw a bird gathering twigs and flying to the neighbouring tree with them to build a nest. In my imagination, the bird was helping clear away dead material to allow new leaves to form. I got up, walked around our garden, and saw numerous other exchanges between life forms: a soft lemon that was dissolving into the soil, the outer leaves of a cabbage that had large holes from a caterpillar's meal. There were even bumblebees hovering inside bright red poppies. Well, it was spring.

This may not have been the first time I properly and profoundly noticed just how much interdependence there is in nature. I suspect my feeling of discovery was a product of my building obsession with theories about the deeper nature of life, in combination with the week's events in which my hopes of winning had been relentlessly mocked. And the realisation made me intensely happy. Everything still had its identity – I did not sense that life was one continuous blur, in keeping with claims that the boundaries between individuals merge when you look at them on a microscopic level. But the idea kept popping into my head that life is based on *radical cooperation*. Cooperation fitted because the actions of each life form supported the growth of other forms; and it was radical because these actions were at the root of both individual survival and the functioning of the entire ecosystem.

The idea of radical cooperation started bouncing around my brain and expanding my focus from the importance of my own life to the importance of *life*. I realised that even when I died, what mattered to me would continue. The dread of death is, after all, the unthinkable horror that your world will end. It assumes that your world is equivalent to your existence as a conscious participator and observer. During this experience, my world was *out there* instead of *in here*.

—◦—◦—◦—

What I experienced is the transcendent potential of humans to 'drop or lift ... out of themselves', as the mythologist Joseph Campbell described, or the 'eutierria' referred to by the ecopsychologist Glenn Albrecht, in which 'a deep sense of harmony and connectedness [with nature] pervades consciousness'.[187] I remained a bounded self, but no longer one in which this boundary contained my deepest concern. In poetic terms, my wonder and joy at the radical cooperation I saw was, essentially, love.

Love is at the heart of the infinite values. Radical cooperation is a way of translating this into the mind-set of an infinite player. It involves trying your best to let go of the belief, trained into us by our society's emphasis on self-promotion and self-acquisition, that security lies in what you have cordoned off for you and your descendants. Insofar as security exists at all, it is better understood as lying in how well we cooperate with each other and the natural world in which we are embedded. If you want to be an infinite player here and now – which is your prime opportunity – that involves unilateral disarmament. You will need to let go and give, in the face of numerous disorienting messages that you should be holding on and taking. And you can draw strength from the vision that, generally speaking, life nurtures that which gives life.

As a side note, one of the positive aspects of climate-change rhetoric – at least in New Zealand to date – is that it tends to talk as if we are in this together. We will need to lower our emissions, adapt to more frequent droughts, protect our low-lying areas in preparation for sea-level rise and so on. This may be because climate-change rhetoric in general is not driven by the free-market survival-of-the-fittest complex that promotes individualism. It is a precious, beautiful approach to assume we need to cooperate to get through this one. I just hope that there are enough of us who keep pouring energy into the assumption that *we are in this together*, to keep it from turning into yet another business/real estate investment opportunity that pulls us further apart. Personally, I am trying to stay alert to signs of an individualistic shift, and intend to resist it if it comes. The notion of radical cooperation is a card I have up my sleeve that strengthens my resolve.

–o–o–o–

Radical cooperation also means helping others grow, which is different from helping them survive (although the latter might sometimes be an infinite play). You can help people survive by giving them food when they are hungry or medicine when they are sick. You can also help them survive by training them to play a standard finite game. We do this when we encourage those entering our profession to learn the rules in order to get ahead. Notably, these rules may include not challenging the ways in which our department or organisation exploits others – which is sometimes called 'collegiality' and is *not* to be mistaken for radical cooperation as I mean it here (more on this in the next chapter). We also train our children to survive when we prod them into settling down in its various guises. Helping others grow, on the other hand, is about supporting their creativity, generosity, curiosity, and all those other infinite game qualities. Good teachers, for example, understand this and do it intuitively. What is this young person trying to say? What can I offer or suggest to help them say it?

If you look a little, you will see numerous opportunities to support people's growth, as the world is full of people tentatively, boldly, offering their creativity to us. It comes in the form of knitted baby cardigans on sale at community markets, local theatre performances, environmental and social justice events, novels by writers in our community, a local bakery that has carefully crafted handwritten labels for its wares, poetry readings at the library, and school musicals. When we support these activities, we open up life. When we support the cookie-cutter or high-glamour alternatives, we restrict life; helping to push it into a monotone format. The radical cooperator, I suggest, is like a discerning bumblebee that pollinates only the plants she senses bring vibrancy and colour to the system as a whole.

––o––o––o––

I started this chapter with nature and will end it there too. The infinite game is a human symbol, but the infinite player is in awe of life in all its forms. Radical cooperation is thus also about being a good neighbour to our non-human companions. Children (so often our superiors!) seem to understand this. The psychologist Gene Myers observed that young children assume their pets and other animals are subjective beings that have feelings and concerns.[188] You could say they take it for granted that these creatures are striving to flourish, just as people are. Furthermore, in their desire to be physically close to animals, children pay careful attention to the animal's responses. In a chapter written with Carol Saunders, Myers describes how his 23-month-old daughter Eva learnt to behave with their two cats.[189] With one cat, 'she tries to hold him and lift him or simply lays her head on him'. She learnt not to touch his eyes and nose, as 'he doesn't put up with that'. With the other cat, exhibiting considerable 'self-control', according to Myers, she obeyed his warning snarls and avoided touching him altogether. Now these observations may seem unremarkable, and in one sense they are: we know that children adjust their behaviour in response to animals. But in another sense they show recognition that *any* affectionate relationship, even across species, must be negotiated.

To come back to the notion of radical cooperation, it is possible for people to simply bulldoze their way through the natural world – we have done this on an extraordinary scale in the last century. But that does not buy us intimacy with nature. As long as we are drawn to animals and wild landscapes – which, the evidence suggests, we are – then we must learn to respond to what natural beings are seeking, insofar as we can work that out through our human lens.[190] A radically cooperative stance in this regard is not the same as a romantic yearning for unspoilt environments. It is a practical orientation that assumes all parties must be considered. Ideally, we would have laws, such as the 'Ecocide law' proposed by the British lawyer Polly Higgins and others, that formalise this consideration.[191] But short of that (and we may always be short of that), we can still develop our own capacity to be in partnership with nature, rather than assume a paternalistic or authoritarian position.

Radical cooperation is not an insipid, self-sacrificial martyrdom, in which you only give and consequently run down your own emotional and material resources. You must care for yourself and your family. Cooperation comes from a place of strength in which you assume you have something to offer. In a gentler world, and in more gentle oases in our current world, this is helped by others' nurturing, which provides recipients with the self-assurance and trust to focus outward. In the world that many of us live within, the player striving to cooperate as deeply and broadly as possible may, ironically, often feel alone and foolish. That is the deal, I am afraid – you give, you feel awkward, and then you sometimes find, as if by magic, that something comes back to you. Not sackfuls of money or a winner's trophy as in – *do good and you will get rich!* – but the warmth of feeling that your life matters because it goes beyond its limited little self.

Chapter Nine

Beware the Trickster

Let me introduce the trickster. The trickster is, in large part, why the infinite game is so, well, *tricky*, and why we cannot just make one move after another, confident that what looks like success *is* success. (For simplicity, I will refer to the trickster with male pronouns, but this is not intended to imply that his tricks are particularly masculine. A consistent gender was needed and somehow 'she' or 'they' did not sound quite right. Make of that what you will!)

The trickster is a master of illusion. He hides inside us and in the spaces between us. His role is to confuse us and set us off in entirely the wrong direction if he can. He is very, very hard to detect. In fact, he can often only be seen in retrospect, like a star whose light does not reach Earth until it has ceased to exist. We know he has been present when we find ourselves in the midst of games that leave us unhappy, in conflict with each other, and destroying the natural world. Once he has thrown us off course in this way, it takes only the lightest touch for him to ensure that we stay under his spell. For once we are immersed in such games, it is as if we are mice on a wheel, we just keeping going and going. Now we must be jolted back to awareness; to the realisation that life could be different.

People across the ages have invented names for the trickster. These include 'diablo' which is related to the Greek 'diaballein' and means to throw across. Alistair McIntosh described diablos as making 'shadow strikes' that trip us up; as he also wrote, 'these reveal the "diabolic" as that underhand dynamic that trips up right relationship'.[192] From a play perspective, Johan Huizinga referred to 'false play' that 'may be used consciously or unconsciously to cover up some social or political design'.[193] There are also bad faeries, fearful gods, devils and demons. They all have illusory abilities, meaning that at least some people at any one time are under their spell. People have created numerous strategies to detect and dispel the trickster. More violent strategies include wars to stamp out evil, witch hunts, executions and exorcisms. More peaceful ones include meditation, psychotherapy, religious texts, social movements, books and films, and most popular of all – conversations with each other to try and figure out what is going on and what to do about it.

Despite our best efforts, the trickster cannot be destroyed. The trickster is part of the infinite game. In fact, paradoxically, while he leads us astray, knowledge of his existence prevents us from being too sure of ourselves and so thinking we have *the* answer. But it still helps to identify some of the more obvious tricks he plays in the minds of people trying their best. Contemplating these can help focus our efforts and avoid some of the self-defeating, infinite-game-disrupting, divisive plays that he dangles in front of us. Below I have outlined five of the trickster's moves for your consideration. These are: insisting that we must win a particular game before we play the infinite game; using infinite rhetoric to hide finite games; encouraging groups of players to break away from the infinite game and pretend they are still playing; fooling people into identifying a trickster that can be destroyed; and pretending there is no infinite game.

Trick one: Insisting that we must win a particular finite game before we play the infinite game

Trick number one goes something like this: when I have got a permanent position/made a million dollars/paid off my house/lost weight/become CEO/got the Nobel Prize/retired, *then* I can consider infinite plays. This is such a crude trick – to tell you that the infinite game is only open to you when you are a finite game winner – that it is hard to believe it works, but it does. To understand it, we need to remember that whenever we play a finite game to win, we are flirting with danger. This danger is what gives finite games their drama. I've seen this in the dart games that participants play in Infinite Game workshops. When they are told that the purpose of game two is to win, people often sit on the edge of their chairs and look at each other, eyes darting around the circle. If someone gets up and begs others for darts, everyone laughs. We are in the delicious state of anticipation that, as Pooh Bear observed, comes just before you eat the honey. To truly enjoy a finite game, you need to take it seriously.

Here's a second example. Decades ago, I remember watching a friend get increasingly bad-tempered and eventually morose while watching a game of rugby in which New Zealand was losing to Australia. 'Why does the score matter so much to you?' I asked. 'Can't you just enjoy the game?' 'Niki,' he replied gravely, 'an essential part of the enjoyment comes from caring about the outcome.'

So it is with all finite games. By playing them seriously, we also undertake to care how they turn out. Ideally, we can hold them lightly as suggested earlier and shake off our wins and losses after a short period of gloating or mourning. But the danger is that by losing ourselves inside the game in order to play it well, we end up staying there. We become enticed by the adrenaline, the glory, and the feeling of belonging that comes from being on a winning team. Or, if we are a loser, we become obsessed with designing moves that will ensure we win next time around. Here is the nub of the problem: we may do this with a vague awareness that this particular game is keeping us from what matters, but something keeps us hooked in nevertheless. This is the trickster in play. He whispers: 'Of course this game is not the point. Just one (more) win and you can quit and do what really matters.' To truly ignore his devilish ways, we must step forward with dignity no matter whether we win or lose.

You do not have to amass a personal fortune in order to critique the financial system. You do not have to be in the top ranks at work to put forward ideas for change or to help others grow and develop. I did not have to be the mother of a winning student in order to write to the principal of my daughter's school and suggest they stop giving end-of-year prizes. In fact, it may be when you lose that you get deeper insight into exactly how the game functions. It was not until my youngest daughter did not get a prize one year – much to her and my disappointment – that I really understood how hurtful the whole system was. Furthermore, I realised that it mostly hurt the young people who liked school – those who tried hard to please their teachers and were nearly good enough to be declared winners. Because I did not write to the school to tell them my daughter had been unfairly overlooked (which was not my call), but to point out more structural problems with prize-giving, I was respectfully heard out.

So when you believe there is a game you must win *before* you can take infinite action, you are probably under the spell of the trickster. Stay there if you like, but – as you well know – your time to play is now.

Trick two: Using infinite rhetoric to hide finite games

Understand this: almost everyone has a feel for the infinite game. Winners of high-profile finite games certainly do. It is perfectly possible, indeed frighteningly instinctive, for finite players to reach for infinite rhetoric in order to make their games more palatable. If you allow yourself to simply accept infinite rhetoric as sign enough that infinite values are in play, the trickster is at work. For example, every political party in New Zealand refers to 'freedom' and 'healthy children' and various other goods. This does not necessarily mean that every political party has the same underpinning commitment to the infinite game as I have described it in this book. The devil, as they say, is in the detail. It is in the policy documents, the actions taken, and how the party responds to new information and feedback.

The really hard problem here is that infinite play is a fuzzy rather than a pure category. While there might be some moves that are clearly infinite play or clearly finite play, a lot of moves are harder to categorise. This is further complicated by the importance of the player's motivation when deciding what is going on. It can be extremely difficult to know one's own motives – let alone be able to infer someone else's. Everyone has surely had the experience of saying to themselves in frustration: 'Why did I do that?!' (speak cruelly, ignore a person in distress, not support someone advocating a position you agree with at a meeting . . .). When it comes to others, especially distant others, it is nearly impossible to know what is going on. Do, for example, the makers of Coca-Cola actually believe that their product contributes to human wellbeing by the pleasure it brings when people drink it? Do powerful advocates of the free market, capital punishment and the war on terror seriously think that these strategies make a better world? And if they do think this, is it because they have analysed the situation with care and come to a reasonable decision?[194]

We could flounder endlessly in the sea of infinite rhetoric that disguises finite play, and even conclude that every move is equally good or bad in the end (as Hamlet says, while his world unravels, 'there is nothing either good or bad but thinking makes it so').[195] This, however, is again the trickster's influence. The reason we know for a fact that all moves are not equal is because we know that our own moves differ in the degree to which they draw on infinite or finite values. I know that I am capable of acting out of love or courage and that I am also capable of acting out of fear or greed. I know I sometimes understand a situation well and so what I say is worth listening to. I also know that sometimes I am missing vital information and go ahead anyway, talking as if I have a clue. I know that sometimes I am fast to learn and sometimes it takes me years to understand what later seems obvious. If this describes me, then it must describe others.

The trickster attempts to stop us thinking too hard about the degree to which various plays are centred on a finite game or the infinite game. He wants us to ignore our intuitive streak that may be able to sense the motives behind a game or its likely consequences. He mutters: 'Look, this game promotes justice/fun/opportunity/ecological diversity – can't you see it is worthwhile?[196] Who are you to challenge it on the basis of your moralistic, do-gooder position?' In this guise, the trickster encourages us to stay confused and not to act.

While we can never outwit him completely, we can counter this spell by reminding ourselves that as infinite players we will always be a little confused. We do not have to 'believe' to act – we are entitled to act according to what seems right given reasonable diligence and consideration. And we can always withhold our blessing. In regard to Coca-Cola for example, we can choose not to buy their products, without necessarily condemning them. So, if, despite a certain plausibility to the infinite rhetoric you are being exposed to, you feel it doesn't add up, then do not be intimidated into giving your blessing. And please – try to avoid bullying people into compliance by using infinite rhetoric yourself. Each time words like 'love' and 'compassion' and 'creativity' are spoken without depth, it wears down their power and so plays into the hands of the trickster.

Trick three: Encouraging groups of players to break away from the infinite game and pretend they are still playing

Trick three derives from our psychology as group members. We find it easy to identify with a group, and to consider that acting in the interests of the group is synonymous with acting in the interests of the common good. In a retrospective analysis of the USA's invasion of Cuba at the Bay of Pigs in April 1961, the psychologist Irving Janis concludes that the Kennedy-led team which agreed to the invasion was captive to 'groupthink'. According to Janis, the decision was a 'perfect failure' as the team made numerous miscalculations, overlooked information, and failed to ask critical questions of the CIA representatives who proposed the plan. The key psychological component in groupthink is what Janis calls 'concurrence-seeking'. In relation to the Bay of Pigs Invasion, Janis concludes: 'The concurrence-seeking tendency was manifested by shared illusions and other symptoms, which helped the members to maintain *a sense of group solidarity*.'[197] There they were, invading a neighbouring country, and they allowed their concern for keeping in with each other to override careful process. That is super-scary if you think about it too hard. Kennedy, who, according to Janis, later thought about it very hard indeed, put in place a considerably improved decision-making process during the thirteen days of the Cuban Missile Crisis in October 1962. And as we know, a possible nuclear war was averted.

Nations are obvious examples of groups that can be readily seduced into acting as if preserving and strengthening their country is unquestionably good. We call it patriotism. We are so trained into assuming that nations are natural entities with (in most cases) clear and indisputable boundaries, that patriotism is child's play for the trickster. He uses our penchant for group identity and loyalty, mixes it with infinite rhetoric, and boom, before we know it, we accept that 'there is no bigger task than protecting the homeland of our country', to quote George W. Bush.[198] If you are reading this book there is a good chance you have not fallen for the patriotism ploy, but there are similar ones.

It is not just nations that break away from the larger community of players and are then tricked into thinking they can still play the bigger game by focusing on their group mission. This happens to companies, professional groups, and educational institutions. It also happens within these institutions. It works more or less like this: a small number of people convince the larger community that they have the talent and skills to create something of great importance to the group as a whole. Let's say, artificial trees that can capture and store carbon. The snag is that they require the community's support to do so. On top of that, they must be left alone for long periods to work on their mission. Perhaps they agree to produce annual reports. These show that progress is slower than expected, and more resources are needed to ensure that they can attract the right people and build better machines to help them with their task. But hey, we are talking about a solution to climate change here. Come on, it's going to take a while.

Now, the difficulty is that sometimes these groups do produce something of value to the broader community if we give them resources and leave them alone for a while. But it is all too easy for the group to talk up its own importance, chance of success, and need for funds. The trickster is whispering to them: 'You have to exaggerate a little or they will not understand. You are making a contribution. Just keep at it. Go on, ask for more and see what happens. Besides which, people's jobs are on the line now. You have got to keep up the narrative for their sake.' And then he darts over to whisper to the rest of the community: 'These people are *specialists*. They need to be paid a lot of money and given a lot of resources. It is too complicated for you to understand, so trust them.'

All of us hear this latter whisper – isn't it why drugs and lawyers are so expensive? And, often, we are too far in the dark to do much except sigh, suspect a hoax, and, if we can, withhold our blessing. But, if *you* are the expert, or work for experts and hear the trickster's whisper, it is time to reflect on whether your group's contract with the rest of the community is still valid. Are you really doing the best you can to contribute to living well together, or are you hiding sadder truths behind the gloss of prestige? Is it time to emerge from your tower and reconnect with the larger community? Each little act of greed, deception, or denial that is hidden under loyalty to a group is an act of acquiescence to the trickster.

—o—o—o—

Of course, loyalty is not always bad – if it was, the trickster would not be able to use loyalty to mess with our hearts and heads. It would be ghastly if we did not (mostly) keep our friends' secrets, forgive our relatives, put up with (some) of our colleagues' irritating habits, attend our children's concerts, and show those closest to us that they are special. The 'left' is sometimes accused of being bereft of loyalty, and so attacking or abandoning those who are working for the same principles. This is demoralising for those trying to build a better world. In the interviews that Sonja Tepavac, Pat Bullen and I did with political activists, every one of them had experienced considerable hurt from their supposed allies. For many, this is what they mentioned when asked about the 'worst thing' about being an activist. For example, one said: 'The worst things that have happened to me in my activist life have been about when you've ended up in a group that's more divided than it was to start with.'[199] These are people who had been arrested, ridiculed in the media, and faced very powerful opponents. So good loyalty is valuable – it strengthens those in our circle of care.

Still, there is a fine line between good loyalty and that which serves to maintain privilege and suffering. Keeping secrets that damage someone else (particularly the secrets of the powerful), misleading others in order to attract resources to your group, and ignoring bullying are examples of the latter. That is not caring, even though the trickster may try and call it such; that is a reluctance to be 'the troubler of the peace' as Alistair McIntosh has put it.[200]

Even if you know that there is something rotten in the state of your group, the trickster can continue to point you towards inaction. 'Pick your battles' is one of his favourite expressions, or, 'This is too small an issue to bother about'. When you fear you will be ostracised for speaking out, this is a comforting mantra to fall back on. We do have to pick our battles. But I am not convinced that any issue is too small when it concerns ongoing misrepresentation or misuse of power. You as an insider are far better placed to know what is happening than onlookers. If by protecting 'one of us' you harm 'one of them', then you are favouring the finite.

—◦—◦—◦—

If you do not feel safe to speak out, you may well be right. The holders of power are unlikely to welcome critique – again, remember that the revolution will not be funded. But if you have decided that enough is enough, then learn from the trickster. Try whispering your concerns to others and see if they agree. Then bide your time until the next consultation process, budget round, planning meeting, or whatever it is that feels like an opportunity to speak out. Even if you are ignored, at least you have given infinite values a moment in the sun. If it feels right to stay with the group, another opportunity will arise and you can do it all again. It's a long, slow game.

Trick four: Fooling people into identifying a trickster that can be destroyed

As I discussed at the beginning of this chapter, the trickster appears across cultures. When he is understood as a mere symbol that allows us to talk about the struggle to do what is right, he is safe from idolatry. But when he is identified as something real we are in trouble. We now have an idol (or an anti-idol) that must be destroyed. This idol, oh so conveniently, distracts us from acknowledging that the struggle is not just out there, but also in ourselves.

It is easy to mock the naivety or shudder at the cruelty behind the idols other cultures have created to contain the trickster. How could the people of Salem have accused some 200 of their townsfolk of witchcraft and hanged nineteen people for this reason in 1692? Why did so many Chinese youth rally behind Mao Zedong's call to purify the nation of bourgeois revisionists during the cultural revolution of the 1960s and 1970s? But as we get closer to our own social setting, it is harder to recognise these idols. Searching for supposed 'evil' is a good place to look. Hitler, communism, the Taliban, ISIS perhaps? Or, for the more left-wing amongst us, how about right-wing politics, neo-liberalism, Christian fundamentalism, or corporate capitalism? 'Just destroy that,' whispers the trickster, 'and you've got me!' See what an obvious trick it is? It shifts our attention from the ongoing process of working out how to live well together, to thinking we have identified the core impediment. Because, logically, if we really have nailed the problem, then why not go in with all guns blazing?

I have a particularly personal distaste for this trick, because universities are replete with attempts to identify 'the problem' through various types of critical analysis (case in point: this book). Don't get me wrong – this scholarship is often insightful. But academic scholarship almost always locates 'the problem' elsewhere – it isn't me or my family or friends or colleagues that have created this mess. Sexism, racism, neo-liberalism, even the hierarchical, competitive university, are usually talked of as if they are produced by others. In the case of the last, university academics are positioned as bystanders or victims.

Consistent with this, the middle class who dominate universities (and politics for that matter) tend to get off rather lightly. They are neither accused of greed and corruption like the rich, nor of failing to look after themselves properly like the poor. Is this because being in the middle means they fade into the background? Maybe. It could also be because the scholarly community has fallen for this enticing trick – that the problem must be *elsewhere*.

It is useful to try and identify epicentres from which oppressive practices radiate with extra power. But the follow-up questions of the infinite player are: 'Where does my power lie?' 'How can I use it?' I was so heartened, for example, to hear that members of the Public Service Association at Auckland Council voted for higher earners to take a salary cut if necessary in order to ensure that all members are paid a living wage. That is such a wonderful play. It acknowledges that even if those in the upper echelons get ten times their share, this does not prevent those of us who only get two or three times our share from saying that we would rather have less so everyone is paid enough to live fully.

To believe you have the trickster in your sights and that he is only 'out there', instead of also snuggled in your soul, is to be played. It is to be well played because it is such an appealing idea – that *I* am all good and *they* are all bad. It can help unite those attempting to grow the common good against the problems they see. But it also encourages us to keep our attention on an idol that is almost always the tip of the iceberg, a symptom of something more fundamental to our culture and something we also carry. While we may feel sophisticated and strong as we sock it to the man, we may also overlook moves that are right before us, helping us grow as a community despite 'them'.

My advice: do not let the trickster lure you into believing you have got him.

Trick five: Pretending there is no infinite game

Trick four happens when the trickster suggests certainty: 'Look, there is evil, go get it.' The trickster is equally as likely to exploit uncertainty and that is the essence of trick five. Sometimes the parade of possibilities that the infinite game creates is just too much. Relying on your intuition, being reluctant to name evil, being cautious about loyalty, playing hard but holding the game lightly – give me a break! 'How can you play a game when there are no clear rules?' the trickster tempts. 'Give up. None of us knows what is good from bad. Become a volunteer or join a church if you must. But stay out of the fantasy that there are "better" and "worse" ways to live together on this planet.'

We fall prey to this trick when we take up the trickster's suggestion or its equivalents. This may take the form of concentrating your efforts on personal growth or transcendence, with no plan for getting back into life. As I have noted before, some forms of spirituality can function in this way. If you become addicted to the quest for enlightenment, then you have left the rest of us behind. 'Religion is the opium of the people', Karl Marx wrote, and it can be.[201] Even my favourite Christmas carol, 'Once in Royal David's City', has some disturbing lines: 'Christian children all must be, mild, obedient, good as he . . . And he leads his children on, to the place where he is gone.' These lines sound suspiciously like a call to comply while you are alive and await the bliss of death. Personal growth can be equally distracting, seducing us into thinking that our key task is to cope with the cruelties of the world, rather than kick up a fuss about them.

Relativism is another trap. In some Infinite Game workshops, after everyone has declared their infinite and finite values and laid them down as cards in the space set aside, someone says something like, 'I actually think all the values could go in either space. What are these notions of finite and infinite anyway?' Now, while this can be argued on a metaphysical level perhaps, in reality there is very little overlap between these categories when you ask real people to work within them. For example, I have only ever seen one person – out of thousands – put 'money' in the infinite space, because there is no human wisdom that says money is of ultimate value. We simply know this as people yearning to flourish (see Chapter Two). Yes, all language is problematic, and all social systems create both suffering and joy, but this does not mean that there is no game to be had in trying to improve them. Is there an infinite game? Well, if you can sense it, and know that at some level you have always sensed it (or something like it), then there is. When you doubt, you can listen to the trickster or you can listen to these words from Arundhati Roy: 'A new world is not only possible, she is on her way. On a quiet day I can hear her breathing.'[202] I can hear her breathing too, and that will do me.

———o——o——o———

These mind-games are not the full range of tricks that keep us from the infinite game. I am sure you are familiar with others. All we can do, with appropriate humility and humour, is try our best to notice what the trickster is up to, and work with others to stay as close as possible to the course that we feel is right.

Chapter Ten

Reflect and Learn

Holding finite games lightly, seeking and expressing authenticity, striving for radical cooperation, and outwitting the trickster are wickedly difficult ventures. If they were easy, then there would not be much of a game. There certainly would not be an infinite game with enough obstacles to keep us engaged for as long as we want to play.

Now, to an extent, you can play the infinite game without much oversight. You can smile at a stranger, plant native trees, go on marches for democracy, raise a guide dog puppy, volunteer at the tennis club, become a mentor for a struggling teenager, write letters to the editor, join Amnesty International, or focus your life's work on developing genuinely useful technologies – without attempting to understand either the big picture or your own motivations. This is the spontaneous play that has always sat at the heart of the game.

But if you want to take the game to another level, you need to prepare, act and learn from your actions. You also need external input beyond your own experience and observations. It is like when you go to a birthday party centred on something new to everyone – say a game of paintball where you are armed with paint-shooting guns and put into teams. At first, as you are all standing there dressed in old T-shirts and holding your guns and helmets, it looks as if everyone is equally equipped to play. It soon becomes apparent, however, that this impression is an illusion. Some are fast, others have great aim or are able to sense what is happening around them, and some – after a few mistakes – manage to bring all the elements of the game together. Others keep adjusting their helmets, are surprised when someone sneaks up on them, hesitate when it is time to shoot, and are out before they have scored.

The rules of paintball might be new to everyone, but some are much better prepared because the skills that make a good player are skills they have cultivated much of their lives. The infinite game is much more complex than running around a forest attempting to splatter your opponents with paint, but you can learn to be a better player – if you pay attention to becoming so. And, after all, you are the one set piece that you must work with every time you make a move. I used to cherish that knowledge as a child – that whatever happened, I would be there to help me through it. Now, I have to admit, I find myself a bit of a nuisance much of the time. But, help or hindrance, I am stuck with me and you are stuck with you.

––◇––◇––◇––

Assuming that I have convinced you – or you already knew – that there is something to be worked on here, how best do you do this? Here is my answer: In whatever way you can, you find places and develop practices in which you can take pause, gather knowledge, and grow yourself. And you nurture those places and practices – thinking of them not as sites of inaction but as the foundation of action. I really need to stress this – that reflecting is not a lazy way to avoid moving forward; it is a crucial part of untangling ourselves from the dominant cultural patterns that are so easy to replicate when we 'just do it'. Reflecting takes skill or else it is simply a form of relaxation (which is no bad thing), or an endless critique that revolves only around itself. I am now going to discuss three possible reflection strategies: the mind-fast, exposing yourself to inspiring ideas, and reflecting with like-minded groups that challenge you to play better.

The mind-fast

The mind-fast is based on an essential feature of reflection – that you must distance yourself from life as usual. Its premise is that if you remove yourself from your usual cultural feed or purge your mind of habitual thoughts – or an extreme stimulus does it for you – stillness will enter. That stillness is assumed to have transformative power, akin to floating above the world and landing somewhere better. Examples include structured retreats or journeys that offer silence, meditation, intense physical activity, forays into the wilderness, walking to a religious site, or ingesting mind-altering drugs.

You can also construct your own version. Two years ago I did a three-day solo hike in the native forest on the outskirts of Auckland. It was June, so our winter; and I took no books or other forms of entertainment. I camped each night in empty campsites and was in bed by 6 p.m., by which time it was pitch black. I set out after I had sent the idea for this book to an agent and he turned it down. This rejection sent me into a crippling crisis of confidence, and I felt I needed to reassess the entire project. I took a notebook and spent a few hours writing alternative outlines, but on the last morning what kept coming to me was the title of Susan Jeffers' 1987 book: *Feel the Fear and Do It Anyway*. I did not have a new outline or any more confidence than when I set out, but I knew I was too far down the line to back out. It had to be done, if for no other reason than to clear the space for something else.

Variations on the mind-fast are an ancient form of reflection and are very widely practised. Practices such as meditation have been advocated by ecopsychologists as a tool for developing authenticity and a means of connecting to nature in a world that discourages both.[203] Mind-fasts are similar to the observer position I discussed as a strategy for holding finite games lightly – they allow you to step out of the fray for a while. Some such experiences may act like an electric shock, giving you a jolt that dislodges the mantras that have been holding you back.

However, as I warned when discussing the observer position, emptying the mind is not a substitute for playing, and neither is it enough to be considered active, engaged reflection. Our minds abhor a vacuum – ultimately they have to settle around some philosophy or other. Furthermore, they rarely just float to somewhere suitable without a bit of prodding. This is where exposing yourself to inspiring ideas comes in.

Expose yourself to inspiring ideas

The underlying premise of exposing yourself to ideas that are likely to challenge and inspire you is that these will push you towards that which you (and people in general) most deeply value. It is a mind-*feast*, if you like, motivated by a sense of seeking to understand how life works and how you could live better. Churches and other faith-based settings offer such stimuli through sermons, prayers and holy books that are designed to engage members with the church's teachings. I think university study can function in this way too – as a time to be apart from real life and to try out new theories, concepts and philosophies. I certainly came across profoundly challenging ideas when I was an undergraduate in psychology, anthropology and English literature. These keep nudging me: Herbert Marcuse's notion of capitalism as absorbing all contradictions, meaning that identity politics must be extremely careful to avoid aiming for equality; our tendency towards diffusion of responsibility and conformity that runs so deep we usually don't notice when we are passing the buck and following the crowd; that languages have a varying number of colour words but these words are developed in a set pattern – if there are just two words, they will be black and white, and if there are three, red/yellow will be added, the latter also being the most colourful colour; the poet who made a billboard stating: 'Anxiety is Vigilant'.

Of the three means of reflection focused on in this chapter, exposure to ideas is the one that I do most easily. I never tire of reading and listening to insights about the human condition. Most of what I come across now is the same old stuff really – but each slight variation makes me feel as if I have finally caught it – something fundamentally true about us that is just what I need to be able to live with joy, compassion and courage. Sometimes it is even my own insight that brings about the thrilling sense that I have broken through the murk. That feeling never lasts, which is why I need to keep reading and listening. Even a terrific idea in this sense is like a new coat; it eventually becomes part of my familiar wardrobe and so does not provide quite enough tension to move me forward.

Note that ideas-based reflection as I mean it does not involve measuring yourself against every new insight and developing an action plan in light of it. It is more about exposing yourself to the thinking of people who have deeply researched or reflected on the issues that concern you, with an attitude of open-mindedness and possibility. In fact, the more deeply an idea 'takes', the less you need to actively apply it. This is explained by the psychoanalyst James Hillman.[204]

> When we do not get an idea, we ask 'how' to put it in practice, thereby trying to turn the insights of the soul into actions of the ego. But when an insight or idea has sunk in, practice invisibly changes ... The only legitimate *How?* in regard to these psychological insights is: 'How can I grasp an idea?' ... Every theory we hold practices upon us in one way or another, so that ideas are always in practice and do not need to be put there.

In other words, if you fully grasp the importance of, let's say, inviting others in, then you will invite others in, as, if you do not do so, then you have not grasped the importance of this idea. It does not follow, however, that ideas 'take' easily and that absorbing them is an exclusively intellectual pursuit. It is more that if you are looking for a formula for inviting others in – or for any of the other infinite game principles discussed in this book – you are looking in the wrong place. As with any other idea about how to live, you need to see the world through it, and when you do, action will follow.

To stick with the current example, if I run a community meeting with an intention to invite others in, I will see a constant flow of opportunities. First, there will be the newcomers who can be greeted with friendship and introduced to someone who will chat with them until the formal business begins. Then there will be discussions that are relevant only to a few members that I can suggest be held another time. I can try to use inclusive language and vary my examples in an attempt to be relevant to everyone. I can invite specific people to speak, and ask every so often if those who have not spoken have something to contribute. At first these gestures may seem awkward, but if inviting people in is truly my aim, I will eventually learn to make them with more grace or to find other gestures that fit better with who I am and the circumstances I am in.

In addition, now that inviting people in is in my sights, I am aware of how others manage to deeply welcome all-comers. I have noticed, for example, that in Māori settings food is always served, and there is an effort to get as many people as possible to gather when the food is blessed. So, in almost all the meetings that I run, food is provided and I offer a secular blessing that acknowledges everyone's value as a human being that has entered our shared space. I am also alert to further explorations of what it means to invite people in when I am reading and listening to thinkers. This is why I latched on to Peter Block's notion that welcoming people means helping them feel that they have '[come] to the right place and are affirmed for that choice'.[205]

Exposure to inspiring ideas, then, gives us the kick-start we need to move beyond business as usual. Without this kick-start, we will probably go on seeing the world as the status quo hands it to us. Like any stimulus, the efficacy of a single input reduces over time. It is extremely unlikely you will hear one good idea and that is all you need. Even the infinite game, which is a very good idea in my view, only lives for me because I have obsessively read around it and continue to discuss it and connect it to related concepts. It remains vigorous for me, because I feed it, often. And because I have the infinite game (Niki's little helper – it can be yours too!), I am, I hope, better at supporting liberating and nurturing practices than before.

To conclude this section: find sources of intellectual nourishment that give your mind something to play with. The aim here is to grow towards that which you value, and so pick books, podcasts, talks, university courses, and so on that seem to come from a values base. You may, at times, want comforting, easily absorbed words – from prayers, manifestos, or popular songs – but I also suggest you try more difficult material that stretches you beyond the familiar. Without a little novelty, we are prone to fall into a rut, assuming that we have got it, when constantly seeking is part of what it means to be fully alive.

Reflect with a like-minded group on how to play better

My motivation for writing this book was to offer a symbol that captures what we are trying to do when advocating for a world more aligned with human and ecological flourishing. I hope this symbol has 'taken' for you. But beyond that, I hope it has allowed you to have new conversations with others who are similarly restless with business as usual. The first two sections in this chapter concerned reflection that can take place alone and in which you are only accountable to yourself. This section covers reflection with the help of a group.

When we reflect in the company of a familiar group, we strengthen our practice and, perhaps most of all, our resolve to practise. Religious and self-help groups are experts at communal reflection: they bring people together with the understanding that they are imperfect and with the aim of improvement. They acknowledge, at a very fundamental level, that being a good (or sober or 'healthy') person takes work – often excruciatingly difficult work that entails loneliness, patience, and most of all *faith* that it is all worthwhile. Simultaneously, they say to attendees that you are not alone – struggle is the human condition and in gathering together we acknowledge this and support each other to do our (somewhat inadequate) best.

In Christian settings for example, weekly services speak of compassion, truth, humility, and the importance of attending to the poor and perhaps to the environment.[206] Living in a secular world, I am always struck by the forthrightness possible in a religious context. When Rowan Williams, who was Archbishop of Canterbury at the time, visited Auckland for a series of discussions on the environment, he described Anglicans as being 'bound' to protect the living world that God had created.[207] At the session I attended, once he had made the duty of Anglicans clear, everyone present (Anglican or not) was required to talk with those sitting near us about our own engagement with environmental issues.[208]

Self-help settings also challenge participants to be better, with the assumption that this is why people have come along. At an Alcoholics Anonymous meeting, those in attendance are invited to share their progress with the group; in Weight Watchers, participants are weighed and can 'share recipes, tips and weight-loss techniques'.[209] At 'Carbon Conversations', those gathered discuss how they are integrating their awareness of climate change into their lives – for example, by deciding not to fly again.[210]

All these rituals regularly remind people of the ideal they are striving for and provide them with opportunities to articulate how they are attempting to put their values or goals into action. There is a general sense that one's personal behaviour matters – simply because the group as a whole has decided to pay attention to it. Thus, directly and indirectly, they invite reflection that takes account of the whole person. 'I'm an alcoholic,' Sandra says at the AA meeting, as if this is something she carries with her at all times. Simultaneously, listening to others' articulations exposes participants to new possibilities for their own lives, some of which are likely to be within reach given that they are offered by members of their own community. And so, when it works well, the group pushes members towards learning and growth.

—◦—◦—◦—

Such personal reflections are, however, rarely a formal part of secular groups with a common-good focus. The Carbon Conversations example is something of an anomaly. In my experience, secular social justice and environmental groups are extremely reticent about calling on people to align their behaviour with a holistic philosophy. I think there are at least two reasons for this reluctance.

The first reason why secular groups may shy away from personal reflection is that they usually assume the 'real' problems lie outside us, and that we make progress by addressing these. (The trickster's fourth play.) The problem might be sexism, racism, the military-industrial complex, children in poverty, the polluted stream in our community, or fishing practices that are driving endangered dolphins to extinction – but it is not *us*. Particular behaviours are still required of participants – but they are generally those that attempt to directly influence the external world: signing petitions, attending protests, cleaning up the stream, campaigning for changes to fishing regulations, and so on. This creates pressure to be a soldier (or a pawn) in service of the cause. Thinking is undesirable; action directed at external change is required.

This position is intellectually reasonable – which is why it has taken such a strong hold on such groups. It's 'the system' that must change if people as a whole are going to live well together on our shared planet. But it neglects the whole person who is attempting to live in alignment with what she or he most cares about. At an extreme, it can even ridicule the gentle, compassionate urge we have to cause as little harm as possible. I recently had a bizarre conversation with two young men who seemed proud that they bought clothes made in sweatshops and did not bother to recycle, because they weren't wasting time on middle-class 'feel good' niceties, but were instead getting on with the revolution. My efforts on both these fronts were considered a prime example of why the revolution is taking so long. I was not inspired to drop everything and join them.

Second, secular groups focused on social and environmental issues seem fearful that if they call on participants to align themselves with what they seek, everyone will drop out. Each member's commitment is assumed to be tenuous. We can ask you to add activities to your life – the protest march, the stream clean-up – but we cannot ask you to reconsider your life itself. Somehow that is seen as nosey, moralistic, evangelical, or otherwise off-putting. Again, this position seems reasonable at first glance, as groups working for the common good in our individualistic, competitive societies do have a delicate hold on members. In the community groups I have belonged to, most people attend only once or twice and even the regulars (including me) put work or family events before meetings.

In fact, however, reflective moments bring people together and strengthen the sense that this is a community worth belonging to. As a member of sustainability networks in community, high-school and university settings, and the teacher of graduate courses with social-good themes, I find myself being most enriched by gatherings in which we drift into a reflective space. When high-school students start talking about their fears of climate change and their frustration at not being able to get their parents to stop using plastic bags (or whatever it is that captures their feelings of powerlessness), the atmosphere is magnetic. It is as if we are finally, fully, together – not because we all face the particular issue being raised – but because we are acknowledging how deeply personal it is to keep our shared values in play. These spaces have somewhere between one and 20 minutes of run time before they lose their magic and flip into a nauseating sense of wallowing.

So now, at the meetings I run, I try and build in short elements of reflection. When we bless the food, I also speak directly to the struggle and joy it is to be working on these issues, followed by at least a minute of silence in which people are invited to consider what we are attempting to do together and what they are bringing into the space we share. In my graduate class, I offer a variety of different opening rounds – such as one in which everyone speaks for about half a minute on their efforts to integrate a new sustainability-related practice into their lives. The point of these rituals isn't to elaborate in detail on a failure or success as might happen at an Alcoholics Anonymous meeting or in a Catholic confessional. It is to nurture an atmosphere of openness and provide tiny prods towards fuller values-based living. It is also to give the message that you are not alone but are in good company in your efforts to live well.

If we do not reflect, we will either stay within the grooves we have carved for ourselves or drift from one choice to another without the sense that there is some pattern to our lives. It is a delicate balance to stay open and yet rooted. But unless we constantly strive to achieve that balance, we are not fully in the game.

—o—o—o—

And so we are done – well, nearly done. I would now like to bring you back to where we started.

Postscript

Welcome to the Infinite Game

At the Festival of Dangerous Ideas at the Sydney Opera House in 2013, the Irish theologian Peter Rollins talked about the folly of attempting to pursue a sense of completeness. When he finished, the host, Simon Longstaff, asked him to explain the weakness in his own argument. Rollins replied:[211]

> 'The weakness is it's not working for me. I'm sorry to burst your bubble, if you've been listening and thinking how this would be really good – no it's not working for me . . . if I actually had what I am talking about I wouldn't be here! I'd be sitting at home with a drink by the fire enjoying the good life. My own frenetic pursuit of reading and reflecting is my own protection mechanism against the trauma of letting go of this idea that I can be whole and complete and learning to live in that. I am speaking to myself. That's the big trick of this.'

That is my big trick too: that, in a sense, this whole book is my attempt to stay true to something which is a perpetual struggle for me and constantly elusive. *I'm sorry to burst your bubble, if you've been reading and thinking how this sounds really good* . . .The truth is that since my teenage years I have been unable to shake a belief that the status quo is wildly out of kilter and that I am one of those destined to see this and take enlightened action. Simultaneously, I have always known how ridiculous that notion is. Me? Destined? Enlightened? You mean the bumbling, half-baked, wholly inadequate person that came up with that ludicrous notion?

Perhaps feeling that we are charged with ushering in a better world is a virus some of us pick up or maybe it is a faulty gene. Whatever it is, it has its own awful, beautiful, sticky momentum; and so we, or at least I, spend untold amounts of time trying to fulfil our/my unfulfillable destiny – and this includes trying to articulate what that destiny is.

The infinite game, for me, is a lovely thing. It fits so much of what I see and comforts me when I feel overlooked by the great stampede towards life as usual. It gives me a sense that I am part of something when I try to be compassionate and generous. But, ultimately, it is a plaything, a symbol, an offering. It is my attempt to take the poetry of James P. Carse and elaborate it into a series of forms that, with a bit of luck, have resonated with you. I have certainly seen hundreds of people respond to the notion of the infinite game and finite games in my workshops and in conversations, and heard them interpret and extend these metaphors in ways that encourage me to think that it is a symbol worth sharing.

Nevertheless, this book must end on a note of humility. There are numerous ways to describe what it means to be human, what it means to live well together, and what it means to actively try and help us live well together. The infinite game is simply one of these. At best, it is the same old wisdom applied to our times, and packaged through a new lens that reveals to those who encounter it some of what has been, previously, hidden from view. It is not a resting point, let alone an ideology. It leaves the next move up to you: if you choose to accept its challenge.

—o—o—o—

Welcome to the infinite game.

Author's Note

As noted previously, the central symbols in this book were inspired by James P. Carse's *Finite and Infinite Games: A Vision of Life as Play and Possibility*. After I heard his brief description of these games on the CBC Radio podcast *Ideas*, I read and re-read his book, underlining key insights and taking notes in the usual manner of scholarly investigation. One of these insights is that infinite players '*initiate* actions of their own in such a way that others will respond by initiating *their* own'. In other passages he made it clear – or at least I read it as clear – that symbolism and stories are invitations to those who encounter them to find and speak as their own 'genius'. For example, he suggested that when writing *The Republic*, Plato was 'fully aware that the entire opus was an act of play, an invitation to readers not to reproduce the truth but to take his inventions into their own play, establishing the continuity of his art by changing it'.[212]

These, and Carse's many other references to art being a stimulus and not an artefact, seemed to urge readers to treat *his* symbols as playthings, devices, inspiration; and not as set pieces that claimed, by having described these games, to bind them to a particular interpretation. In other words, to take him seriously, one had to not take him too seriously.

I loved this invitation to break away from an academia that has become stymied by the need to account for every thought by tracing its origins to the published thoughts of someone else or to empirical evidence. That game, the game of academic rigour as it is currently played in the social sciences, is like any finite game – useful to a point, but not *the* point. It can be like wading through a mudflat trying to grasp hold of mangrove shoots and drag them in your wake. You may become so bogged down by the task that you forget what you really wanted to explore. And that is a terrible shame when, to use the words of the philosopher Roberto Unger (and hence play the very game I am critiquing!), we as social scientists are called on to provide 'insight' into what is now and 'imagination' for the 'adjacent possible'.[213] We are not called upon to keep our self-imposed rules, except insofar as they enrich and deepen our capacity for insight and imagination – and the ability to express what we come up with to others.

So, after my initial close readings of Carse's book, I constructed the pairs of statements that contrast the two types of games, and designed the Infinite Game workshops. The statements were modified a great deal over time as I conducted workshops and began writing the book. I also realised, the more I kept reading, writing and sharing these ideas, that I had to let go of my notes on how Carse conceptualised these games. The project would only work if I stopped concerning myself with where Carse stopped and I started. These symbols needed to become mine and not an application or adaptation of Carse's symbols.

What this means is that the book you have read is an original conception of the infinite game and finite games. It is not original in the sense that it is wholly unique; it is original in the sense that it originates from me – and everything that has made me see life as I do, including Carse's book. If I have not been clear, or contradicted myself, this isn't because I have 'misread' Carse.

Anyone who is interested is encouraged to read *Finite and Infinite Games*. It is an extraordinary book, and very different to this one. Notably, although it has quotations, it has no references, despite it being rich with ideas from philosophy, psychoanalysis and religious texts. If the medium is the message, then perhaps the style of *Finite and Infinite Games* is one reason why I sensed Carse really meant what I thought he meant. That is why I end my book with the same invitation.

Appendix

Infinite Game Workshop Outline

Since 2012, I have run over 90 Infinite Game workshops. Thirty were part of a formal research study. The detailed findings from these workshops have been described in two academic publications.[214] The findings are also scattered throughout this book along with less formal observations. The workshops evolved over time and have a flexible structure that varies according to the number of participants, the setting, and how much time is available. They usually take between 45 and 90 minutes. I've run workshops with as few as eight participants and as many as 200.

In the most common variation, which works for up to about 30 people, participants sit on chairs in a circle. I place a cloth on the floor in the middle of the circle. Each person is given a game sheet, eight blank coloured 'cards' to write on, and a piece of scrap paper for making a paper dart (or aeroplane). One side of the game sheet has a list of paired statements that describe the infinite game and finite games. The latest version of this list can be seen in the Introduction to this book (see p. 8); it changed considerably over time. The other side of the game sheet has instructions for each part of the workshop and space for participants to write responses.

As people arrive, I often encourage them to make a paper dart with their scrap paper and to ask for help from another participant if they need to. It gives everyone something to do, and is an easy way to make conversation with others while they wait for the workshop to begin. Once everyone has arrived, I welcome participants to the game and ask them to state their first name only. Infinite players, I say, bring only their names. In some workshops, participants are then asked to write down on one of their cards their work, family details, where they are from, and anything else they might otherwise share in an introductory round. They do not share these details, but simply put their completed card into a box by the door. I state that this further signifies how, just for this workshop, we are leaving these markers of our differences at the door. Next, we go around the circle, with each participant in turn reading one statement pair from the list on their game sheet, until all the statements have been read. Sometimes this means participants may read more than one pair, or that the statements may run out before the participants do. In the latter case, I usually get the remaining participants to start reading again from the top of the list.

I then use the cricket metaphor, described in the Introduction, to further tease out the differences between finite games and the infinite game. Next, I note that finite games and the infinite game are played with different values – this is the second characteristic listed on their game sheet. I read out an 'instruction card' that defines what is of infinite value and place it in the middle of the cloth. Things of infinite value are defined as: 'Sacred, precious or special; of value for their own sake. They make the world truly alive. Things of infinite value can be in any dimension: an emotion, a relationship, part of the natural world, a quality or an object.'

This definition is also on the game sheets. Each participant is asked to write down three things of infinite value, each on one of their coloured cards. They do this without talking, to ensure that they provide an intuitive, felt response rather than checking with others that they are on the right track. Participants are able to ask me questions if they want further elaboration. I resist giving examples, either when talking to the group or to individual participants who are not sure they have understood the definition correctly. When everyone has written on their cards, they stand up one by one, read their cards aloud and place them on the cloth in the middle. I encourage the first person to spread their cards out and subsequent people to lay each of their cards near one that is similar, so themes or clusters start to appear.

Participants are then shown a copy of the infinite values word cloud that can be found in Chapter One (see p. 38). I tell them that this represents the infinite values offered by over a thousand people in previous workshops. Next, they are invited to discuss the infinite values exercise. Usually they do this first in small groups of three to five participants and then with the workshop as a whole. There is space on the game sheet to record their small-group discussion. After this, the same process is repeated in relation to things of finite value. The instruction card and the participants' contributions are, however, placed on the outside of the cloth. The infinite values cards remain visible throughout. Finite values are defined as those things that have worth: *'because of what they signify or enable. They may be of value only to a particular group of people who deem them so. They can be in any dimension: an emotion, a relationship, part of the natural world, a quality or an object.'*

After discussing the finite values exercise, participants play three dart games. If some people have not yet made a paper dart, time is allowed for this. I am careful to invite participants to take a role in these games – to experiment with how they would like to behave. This is partly to encourage people to loosen up, but also to reduce the possibility that players will be judged for their actions. The object of each dart game is given on an instruction card which I read aloud and place in the middle of the cloth – on top of the infinite values instruction card. The dart game instruction cards are as follows:

Game one: The object of this game is to keep the darts in play and include other players.

Game two: The object of this game is to win. The winner is the person with the most darts. You may not grab a dart from another person. You may not manufacture new darts.

Game three: The object of this game is to be on the winning team. The winning team must be three people. The winning team is the team with the most darts. You may not grab a dart from another person. You may not manufacture new darts.

I let game one run for about five minutes. At the end of this game, I collect any darts that are on the floor and give them to participants. I make sure that the darts are not equally distributed – some people might end up with four darts, others none. This is to create an uneven playing field, as is true of life's finite games. I then announce game two. I let this game run until there is obviously a winner or just a few people have most of the darts. Potential winners count their darts in front of everyone. We clap the winner and I hang a plastic gold medal around their neck – all medals are returned at the end of the game.

As soon as the award ceremony is completed, I lay down the instruction card for game three. As with game two, I bring this game to an end when it appears as if just a few teams, or sometimes only one team, has the most darts. As game three tends to result in huddles of players negotiating who will be on the winning team, I sometimes ask for a pause in the game to check what is happening inside these huddles and how close they are to putting forward a team. The winners of game three are also clapped and receive plastic gold medals.

After the dart games, participants have the opportunity to discuss what they observed, and how they acted and how they felt. Usually this is first done in small groups and then with the whole workshop. There is space on the game sheet for participants to make notes. I almost always have to draw this component to an end before the conversation has run out, as the dart games prompt a great deal of discussion.

The workshop ends in different ways. Sometimes I show participants a drawing of Morpheus, from the 1999 film *The Matrix*, offering Neo – the main character – a red pill or a blue pill. The red pill, I say, gives entry to the real world, with all its tensions and decisions that have consequences. The blue pill means slipping back into the status quo, unaware of how finite games and the infinite game are in play. I then hand around a tin with two compartments. One is full of red jellybeans and the other blue jellybeans. Participants help themselves to one or the other. I try to get people talking to each other during the passing of the jellybeans, so that attention is not on the participant with the tin in front of them. (The red jellybeans need replenishing much more frequently than the blue!) Sometimes, as well as, or instead of, giving them an opportunity to pretend they are Keanu Reeves deciding whether to be ripped from the Matrix, I ask them to write on one of their cards if and how they intend to carry awareness of these games forward in their lives. They do not declare their intention aloud but simply put their card into a box in the middle of the cloth. If the workshop is within a single organisation or involves a single interest group (for example, teachers), it usually ends with discussion of how these games apply in their context and how they could adjust their finite games to keep the infinite game in play. I modify the game sheet to create questions to prompt this discussion, which is usually first in small groups and then extended to the workshop as a whole.

Throughout each workshop, I am careful to create what I feel are infinite game conditions – insofar as the context allows. If the workshop is independent of a bigger event (such as a conference), I make sure there is food provided. I try to tidy the space if needed, so the circle of chairs is not lost amongst a clutter of other furniture. The cloth I use is full of colour. I watch very carefully for who wants to speak so that the larger discussions are not dominated by just a few voices. Please go to the Infinite Game website, www.infinite-game.net, for more information.

––o–o–o––

For a manual that outlines exercises to explore the concepts in this book and Niki Harré's book *Psychology for a Better World* please go to http://www.press.auckland.ac.nz/NikiHarreManual.

Notes

1 Carse (1986). See the Author's Note (p. 183) for a discussion of the relationship between Carse's book and this one.

2 A second edition of this book came out in 2018 under the title *Psychology for a Better World: Working wih People to Save the Planet.*

3 There have been several other attempts to describe what underpins the uncoordinated 'movement' for social change – for example, Paul Hawken's notion of 'blessed unrest' (Blessed Unrest, http://www.blessedunrest.com); and the UK-based Public Interest Research Centre's work on a 'common cause' (Common Cause Foundation, http://valuesandframes.org). On similar lines, Naomi Klein in her book *This Changes Everything: Capitalism vs. the Climate* (2014) and protest marches in a claimed 162 countries under the banner 'To change everything, we need everyone' (People's Climate Movement, http://peoplesclimate.org) have made the connection between climate change and the entire economic and political system.

4 After atheism: New perspectives on God and religion, part 4 – James P. Carse. (2004, July 8). *Ideas.* http://www.cbc.ca/radio/ideas/after-atheism-new-perspectives-on-god-and-religion-part-4-1.2914009

5 See the Appendix (p. 185) for an outline of the workshops. For further details on findings from the workshops see Harré & Madden (In press).

6 See Douglass (2008) for detailed evidence in support of 'secret' communications between the two leaders.

7 Playing the game of life – Alan Watts. (2013, December 11). [Video file]. https://www.youtube.com/watch?v=QXvoYGrnuv8

8 The Seven Kingdoms is the volatile realm located on the continent of Westeros in the medieval fantasy epic *Game of Thrones.*

9 For discussions of the ubiquity of competition in our institutions see Gottlieb (2006); Heffernan (2014); Kelly (2010); Leopold (1949); Russell (1930).

10 For a fuller argument about how this version of the theory of evolution dominates Western thinking see Nowak (2011); Tudge (2013).

11 The urge to be altruistic towards close relatives is known as the kin selection hypothesis.

12 The 6 killer apps of prosperity – Niall Ferguson. (2011, July). [Video file]. http://www.ted.com/talks/niall_ferguson_the_6_killer_apps_of_prosperity?language=en

13 Nowak (2011), p. xiii.

14 Exploring how and why trees 'talk' to each other – Suzanne Simard. (2016, September 1). [Video file]. http://e360.yale.edu/feature/exploring_how_and_why_trees_talk_to_each_other/3029/

15 The American Society for Microbiology's estimation of the proportion of bacteria in our bodies can be found here: Humans have ten times more bacteria than human cells: How do microbial communities affect human health? (2008, June 5). *ScienceDaily.* http://www.sciencedaily.com/releases/2008/06/080603085914.htm

16 For a fuller discussion of this, particularly in regard to the USA, see Stucke (2013).

17 The 'level playing field' was used by the USA government on the following website: Office of the United States Trade Representative, https://ustr.gov/tpp/ (accessed 11 October 2015).

18 These quotations were obtained from the following websites: NZ National Party, https://www.national.org.nz/news/news/media-releases/detail/2015/10/05/PM-welcomes-TPP-as-NZ-s-biggest-trade-deal; Office of the United States Trade Representative, https://ustr.gov/tpp/; Channel News Australia Business, http://www.channelnewsasia.com/news/business/australia-hails-tpp-as/2172478.html (all accessed 11 October 2015).

19 Acemoglu & Robinson (2013).

20 See Rivlin (2016) for a report on how companies get access to shelf space in supermarkets in the USA.

21 Hampden-Turner & Trompenaars (1997).

22 For a developed argument about how the decline of the church has led to a collapse of moral authority see Hamilton (2008).

23 Karen Armstrong's book *The Great Transformation: The Beginning of Our Religious Traditions* (2006) gives a detailed history of the Axial Age.

24 James (1902), p. 476.

25 Armstrong (2006).

26 de Almeida (2007), p. 191; see also McIntosh (2001/2004) for references to 'the God of Love' (p. 117); Thomas Merton (1965/1979) on the importance of Christians actively 'living love'; and Pope Francis's 2015 encyclical that is full of references to love and the power of community in overcoming challenging situations.

27 This is also expressed by Hamilton (2008) who says (p. 179): 'If the meaning of human life cannot be grounded in the transcendent, it can only be grounded in the beings themselves.'

28 Pollan (2006).

29 Ryan & Deci (2002). These authors provide an argument for why 'autonomy', which is the equivalent to 'authenticity' as I am using it here, is a vital part of human wellbeing.

30 de Waal (2009); Hollan (2012).

31 Hamilton (2008); Naess (2008), see in particular pp. 82 & 93.

32 Nucci (2001); Turiel (2002).

33 For research on young children's attitudes towards animals and how it changes as the children age see Myers (2007).

34 Kahn, Jr. (2003); the two quotations are from pp. 117 & 119 respectively.

35 Thomas (2003); the passage quoted is on p. 74.

36 As Arne Naess (2008) wrote (p. 210): 'We must as a nation examine what aspects of our way of life we cherish and wish to extend and preserve. Discussion groups, panels, debates, articles, books, essays, radio, and television (and today the Web), on both local and national levels, must be enlisted to facilitate this self-examination.'

37 For further details see Harré, Madden, Brooks & Goodman (2017).

38 Our findings are consistent with research on 'intrinsic' values in psychology that suggest these are derived from basic human needs. Numerous studies

show that such values are associated with personal wellbeing as well as pro-social and pro-environmental behaviour. See, for example, Brown & Kasser (2005); Kasser (2011); Kasser & Ryan (1993); Ku & Zaroff (2014); Sheldon & McGregor (2000).

39. For further details see Harré, Madden, Brooks & Goodman (2017).
40. See Grouzet et al. (2005); Kasser & Ryan (1993).
41. Eisenstein (2011), p. 40.
42. For a well-developed argument along these lines see Blackmore, Underhill, McQuilkin, Leach & Holmes (2013).
43. 'Intellectual challenges' is Adventure Cycles' term (see their website, http://www.adventure-auckland.co.nz/adventurecycles/php/index.php).
44. Foreman (2013), p. 195.
45. INCITE! Women of Color Against Violence (2007). For discussion of the tendency of social movements to reproduce the mechanisms of the status quo see Haiven & Khasnabish (2014).
46. See in particular Hawk (2007); Rodríguez (2007); Rojas (2007); Smith (2007).
47. For the former see Hawk (2007) and for the latter Allen (2007).
48. Woodman (2011).
49. Woodman (2011), p. 55.
50. Woodman (2011), p. 53.
51. Merton (2008), p. 53.
52. Maslow (1970).
53. Piff, Kraus, Côté, Cheng & Keltner (2010).
54. I am not saying there are no works that challenge these concepts, but I do not see these falling into the category of 'enduring human wisdom'. I realise that argument is something of a tautology, but it is difficult to point to such works that have been popular for more than short periods. Even Machiavelli's *The Prince* (1532), which is about gaining power at the expense of compassion, has been argued to be satirical.
55. Block (2008), p. 3.
56. For example, sexism may be 'benevolent' and thus subtle; see Glick & Fiske (1996).
57. Kate McKenzie now only woman CEO in NZX50. (2017, February 21). *New Zealand Herald*. http://www.nzherald.co.nz/business/news/article. cfm?c_id=3&objectid=11804694
58. Freire (1970/1996); Graeber (2013).
59. For descriptions of these processes see, for example, Freire (1970/1996); Graeber (2013); Green (1999); Harré, Bullen & Olson (2006); Hassan (2014); Kahane (2012); Starhawk (2002); van Egmond (2014).
60. De Koven (1978/2013), p. 126.
61. Samuel (2010), p. 11.
62. Cavanaugh (2008), p. 91.
63. So is buying directly from the farmer; see Cavanaugh (2008) for a more detailed argument along these lines.
64. The Coca-Cola website when I visited it was full of upbeat messages about happiness and human connection, (accessed 18 May 2015). http://www.coca-cola.com/global/glp.html

65 Schumacher (1973).
66 Patagonia, https://wornwear.patagonia.com/ (accessed 4 July 2017).
67 Pirsig (1974), p. 319.
68 Huizinga (1950), p. 12.
69 Paxman vs Russell Brand. (2013, October 23). *BBC Newsnight*. [Video file]. https://www.youtube.com/watch?v=3YR4CseY9pk
70 Russell Brand destroys MSNBC talk show host. (2013, June 19). [Video file]. https://www.youtube.com/watch?v=ynUjo99Gzbk
71 Carse (2008); Dicker (2009); Fisher (2002); Fox (1983); Huizinga (1950); McIntosh (2001/2004); Tacey (2009a).
72 Csikszentmihalyi (1975); Nakamura & Csikszentmihalyi (2002).
73 For a fascinating article on motorbike racing and flow in Japanese youth see Sato (1988).
74 Csikszentmihalyi (1975).
75 McGonigal (2011), p. 3.
76 See the Appendix (p. 185) for further details.
77 For more details see Harré & Madden (In press).
78 See, for example, Bardel, Fontayne, Colombel & Schiphof (2010); Wilson & Kerr (1999).
79 Bardel, Fontayne, Colombel & Schiphof (2010).
80 Wilson & Kerr (1999).
81 Kerr, Wilson, Bowling & Sheahan (2005), p. 255.
82 Bloch (2002), p. 123.
83 De Koven (1978/2013), p. 4.
84 Fang & Casadevall (2015).
85 Fang & Casadevall (2015), p. 1230.
86 History of Wikipedia, https://en.wikipedia.org/wiki/History_of_Wikipedia (accessed 4 July 2017).
87 This relates to the concept of extrinsic motivation. If a behaviour is motivated by an external reward, it is unlikely to be maintained if that reward is removed: Ryan & Deci (2000).
88 A very interesting analysis of why non-violent movements succeed more often than violent ones in overthrowing existing regimes is made by Chenoweth & Stephan (2011). They argue that a key advantage of the former is they are more likely to attract wide participation through those involved drawing in others from their social networks.
89 Turner (2007), p. 9 (emphasis in the original).
90 If you have a child that is an extremely fussy eater, please seek advice. Some children may require greater help to eat a range of foods.
91 Yeates & Lehman (2016), p. 8. This has also been taken up by eco-centric environmentalism – for example, Berry (1999).
92 For examples of complexity theory being applied to social systems see Clayton & Radcliffe (1996); Hawe, Shiell & Riley (2009); Olson & Eoyang (2001); Stacey (1996); Vickers (1965/1995).
93 For a comprehensive discussion of complex systems see Capra & Luisi (2014).
94 Taleb (2012).

95 Ministry for the Environment (2015).

96 Household economic survey: Year ended June 2013. (2013, November 28). Statistics New Zealand. http://www.stats.govt.nz/browse_for_stats/ people_and_communities/Households/HouseholdEconomicSurvey_ HOTPYeJun13/Commentary.aspx

97 New Zealand's 2030 climate change target. (2016, December 20). Ministry for the Environment. http://www.mfe.govt. nz/climate-change/reducing-greenhouse-gas-emissions/ new-zealand%E2%80%99s-post-2020-climate-change-target

98 Olson & Eoyang (2001).

99 The concept of attractors is derived from mathematics and physics and has been widely used; it is not original to these authors.

100 Sahlberg (2015).

101 For more details see Blythe et al. (2013).

102 For a report on the waste to landfill diversion project see Western Springs College Waste Minimisation Report, prepared by Waste Not Consulting for Western Springs College and Ministry for the Environment: (2013, March). http://www.westernsprings.school.nz/WesternSpringsCollege_ NewsStories/WSC_Waste_Wise_Report_2013.pdf

103 For an article on the Maui's dolphin litter challenge see Townrow, Laurence, Blythe, Long & Harré (2016).

104 Stutchbury (2013).

105 This theme comes up again and again in writing about current social systems – for example, Eisenstein (2011); Hillman (1989); Wilbur (2001).

106 Jacobs (1961).

107 Jacobs (1961), p. 50.

108 Jacobs (1961); the first quotation in this paragraph is on p. 34 and the second on p. 65.

109 See, for example, Gottlieb (2006); Murphy (2012); Plotkin (2003).

110 This is alluded to by Jamieson (2008) who refers to the wild as unpossessed by people, giving us a sense of freedom.

111 Monbiot (2013).

112 Monbiot (2013), p. 45.

113 For more on the issue of controlling nature and science's role in this see Gottlieb (2006); Tudge (2013).

114 For more on eco-centric environmentalism see Berry (1999); Rønnow (2006); B. Taylor (2010, 2011).

115 Cited by B. Taylor (2010), p. 99.

116 For example, Davis (2012); Dicker (2009); Fisher (2002); Murphy (2012); Noonan & Macken (2009); Plotkin (2008); Tacey (2009a).

117 Berry (1999).

118 Tacey (2009a), p. 366.

119 Plotkin (2008), p. 3.

120 Ecosystems & wildlife under threat. WWF. http://wwf.panda.org/what_we_ do/footprint/agriculture/soy/ecosystems/ (accessed 4 July 2017).

121 Global palm oil demand fuelling deforestation. Worldwatch Institute. http://www.worldwatch.org/node/6059 (accessed 4 July 2017).

122 Global dairy industry 'mooooving' forward. Statistics New Zealand. http://www.stats.govt.nz/browse_for_stats/snapshots-of-nz/yearbook/environment/agriculture/dairy.aspx (accessed 4 July 2017).

123 New Zealand's greenhouse gas inventory 1990–2013. (2015, April). Ministry for the Environment. http://www.mfe.govt.nz/sites/default/files/media/Climate%20Change/nz-greenhouse-gas-inventory-snapshot-2015.pdf

124 Because the computer says so. (2015, June 14). Herald on Sunday. http://www.nzherald.co.nz/nz/news/article.cfm?c_id=1&objectid=11464802

125 For example, Foale, Cohen, Januchowski-Hartley, Wenger & Macintyre (2011) showed that fishing taboos were not to preserve the fisheries but to manage the access of different groups.

126 Anderson (2013), p. 169.

127 Hames (2007); Sayre (2012).

128 The STM Report: An overview of scientific and scholarly journal publishing. (2012, November). STM. http://www.stm-assoc.org/2012_12_11_STM_Report_2012.pdf

129 For example, Eisenstein (2011); Fisher (2002); Kahn, Jr. & Hasbach (2012); Leopold (1949).

130 For an argument that we are not sufficiently socially developed to keep our technological knowledge in its proper place see Wilbur (2001).

131 For extended arguments on this topic see Sheldrake (2013).

132 Ehrlich (2002), p. 34.

133 Diamond (2005).

134 Diamond (2005), p. 329.

135 The world's richest and poorest countries. (2017, February 13). Global Finance. https://www.gfmag.com/global-data/economic-data/worlds-richest-and-poorest-countries

136 These figures are from 2015. Key World Energy Statistics, 2017. International Energy Agency. http://www.iea.org/publications/freepublications/keyword2017 (accessed 26 October 2017).

137 See, for example, The Solutions Project, http://thesolutionsproject.org/, or Energy Transition, http://energytransition.de/ (accessed 4 July 2017).

138 The role of art is highlighted in numerous critiques of modern life, including Dicker (2009); Fisher (2002); Jacobs (1961); Jamieson (2008); McIntosh (2001/2004).

139 de Botton (2002), p. 15. This observation was also made by Andy Warhol and is discussed in M. C. Taylor (2007), and reappeared more recently in the popular 2012 thriller by Gillian Flynn, Gone Girl.

140 Pride (2014): written by Stephen Beresford; directed by Matthew Warchus; produced by David Livingstone.

141 Sewall (2012), p. 280.

142 Dicker (2009), p. 60.

143 J. Campbell (1972); Hillman (1989).

144 J. Campbell (1972), p. 216.

145 Geering (1994), p. 33.

146 Carse (2008).

147 Hamlet, Act III, scene ii, line 128.

148 As cited by Eisenstein (2011), p. 159.
149 Execution of Sarah Harriet Thomas at Bristol. *Trove Digitised Newspapers.*
http://trove.nla.gov.au/newspaper/article/62045132 (accessed 4 July 2017).
150 Bristol's traumatic last hanging and the Gaol's closure. (2001, September 20).
BBC Online. http://www.bbc.co.uk/bristol/content/features/2001/09/20/
new-gaol/new-gaol4.shtml
151 Thanks to Barbara Grant for the example of Sarah Thomas and this
observation, which refers to the book *Women Who Make a Fuss:
The Unfaithful Daughters of Virginia Woolf* by Isabelle Stengers and
Vinciane Despret. Grant (2016); Harré, Grant, Locke & Sturm (2017).
152 See Becker (2013).
153 Erikson (1950), p. 269.
154 For an interesting discussion of how we deny death in various ways, and a list
of some major texts on this issue, see Kets de Vries (2014).
155 Charles Eisenstein (2011) writes this in relation to letting go of the need for
wealth in order to protect us from illness (p. 375): 'Of course you can imagine
various medical emergencies and such in which wealth can be a lifesaver, but
so what? We are all going to die anyway, and no matter how long you live, the
moment will come when you look back upon your years and they seem short,
a flash of lightning in the dark of night, and you realize the purpose of life
is not after all to survive in maximum security and comfort, but that we are
here to give, to create that which is beautiful to us.'
156 Kushner (2004), p. 202.
157 The possibility of letting go, and so being able to focus on what makes
life rich and full, is a common theme in philosophy and theology. For a
compelling example see the writings of Matthew Fox (1983), a Christian
priest and activist.
158 The webpages used for these predictions are: World population to reach 9.7
billion by 2050 new study predicts. (2013, October 2). *The Telegraph.* http://
www.telegraph.co.uk/news/earth/10348822/World-population-to-reach-
9.7-billion-by-2050-new-study-predicts.html; The world in 2050: When the
5 largest economies are the BRICs and US. (2012, February 17). *The Atlantic.*
http://www.theatlantic.com/business/archive/2012/02/the-world-in-2050-
when-the-5-largest-economies-are-the-brics-and-us/253160/; The world:
Life expectancy (2050) – Top 100+. http://www.geoba.se/population.php?pc
=world&type=015&year=2050&st=rank&asde=&page=1
159 Diamond (2005).
160 Gilbert (2006), p. 184. This passage has been slightly rearranged here, as the
first sentence comes last in the original.
161 McIntosh (2001/2004), pp. 123 & 124 (emphasis in the original).
162 Carse (1994), p. 149.
163 Hillman (1989), p. 124.
164 Clance & Imes (1978), p. 1.
165 For a wonderful autobiographical account that takes this perspective
on feeling like an imposter see Karen Armstrong's *The Spiral Staircase:
My Climb Out of Darkness* (2004).
166 Unpublished data.

167 James (1902), p. 347. Eisenstein (2011) makes a similar point in a modern context, p. 89.
168 Gottlieb (2006), pp. 164 & 165.
169 Eisenstein (2016). Eisenstein does not call these 'force-fields' but refers to Rupert Sheldrake's theory of 'morphic resonance'; see Sheldrake (2013).
170 Haiven & Khasnabish (2014).
171 For their website see Rubbish Free, www.rubbishfreeyear.co.nz (accessed 4 July 2017).
172 Huizinga (1950).
173 See, for example, J. Campbell (1972); Carse (2008); Merton (2008).
174 Haiven & Khasnabish (2014), p. 20.
175 Harré, Tepavac & Bullen (2009), p. 340.
176 For an excellent discussion of these issues in relation to evaluating social programmes see D. T. Campbell (1976). Joanna Macey (2007) also offers wisdom in this regard.
177 Thanks to McIntosh (2001/2004), pp. 179 & 180 for this term.
178 This process is described by Eisenstein (2011); Fisher (2002); Marshall (2009); McBride (2009); McIntosh (2001/2004); Tacey (2009b).
179 Fisher (2002), p. 183.
180 Carse (1994), p. 152. This is similar to the concept of 'Quality' in Robert Pirsig's *Zen and the Art of Motorcycle Maintenance* (1974).
181 McIntosh & Carmichael (2016), p. 179.
182 For more on this see Harré (2013).
183 This aspect of authenticity (or similar notions) has been discussed by Fisher (2002).
184 The first of these featured the Netherlands: The Netherlands welcomes Trump in his own words. (2017, January 23). [Video file]. https://www.youtube.com/watch?v=ELD2AwFN9Nc. Denmark followed up with: Denmark second | Denmark Trumps the Netherlands at being no. 2. (2017, February 2). [Video file]. https://www.youtube.com/watch?v=ryppmnDbqJY
185 The first quote is Marshall (2009), p. 214; the second is M. C. Taylor (2007), p. 48.
186 Several writers have commented on this, including Eisenstein (2011); Fisher (2002). From a mythological or religious perspective, Armstrong (2010); J. Campbell (1972) critique historical periods and traditions that have insisted people live by principles or rigid moral rules and ignore their own feelings and ethical responses.
187 The first quote is from J. Campbell (1972), p. 57; the second from Albrecht (2012), p. 259.
188 Myers (2007).
189 Myers & Saunders (2002); the quotations are from pp. 154 & 155.
190 For a discussion of the biophilia hypothesis in relation to children's development see Kahn, Jr. (1997); Kellert and Wilson (1993).
191 Polly Higgins, http://pollyhiggins.com (accessed 4 July 2017).
192 McIntosh (2012), p. 68 & p. 52 respectively.
193 Huizinga (1950), p. 205.

194 See my book *Psychology for a Better World* (2018) for a full discussion of the difference between errors of ignorance and errors of interpretation. It is the latter which we judge to demonstrate a moral breach.

195 *Hamlet*, Act II, scene II, lines 250–51.

196 Or as Bob Dylan writes in his song 'Man of Peace' from the album *Infidels* (1983): 'sometimes Satan comes as a man of peace'.

197 Janis (1983), p. 47 (emphasis added).

198 Remarks at a luncheon for gubernatorial candidate Bill Simon in Stockton. (2002, August 23). The American Presidency Project. http://www.presidency.ucsb.edu/ws/?pid=64884

199 Harré, Tepavac & Bullen (2009), p. 338.

200 McIntosh (2001/2004), p. 181.

201 Karl Marx in the Introduction to *Critique of Hegel's Philosophy of Right* (1843).

202 Confronting Empire – Arundhati Roy. (2003, January 30). *Outlook India*. http://www.outlookindia.com/website/story/confronting-empire/218738.

203 Fisher (2002); Macey (2007).

204 Hillman (1989), pp. 54–55 (emphasis in the original).

205 Block (2008), p. 3.

206 For extensive discussion of this see Armstrong (2006) or de Botton (2012).

207 For the script of a talk Rowan Williams gave around the same time that uses this language see Our duty to the earth. (2009, March 26). *Guardian*. https://www.theguardian.com/commentisfree/belief/2009/mar/26/religion-anglicanism

208 Pope Francis's 2015 encyclical on Care for our Common Home is similarly infused with statements about how 'convictions of our faith' and 'our conversion' as Christians entails profound respect for the natural world.

209 What to expect from Weight Watchers meetings. LoveToKnow. http://diet.lovetoknow.com/wiki/Weight_Watchers_Meetings#LRHmdCm2yqqW0j8b.97 (accessed 4 July 2017).

210 Randall (2009).

211 To believe is human; to doubt, divine – Peter Rollins. Festival of Dangerous Ideas 2013. (2013, November 11). [Video file]. https://www.youtube.com/watch?v=hzkwj7bUvUY

212 Carse (1986). The quotes in this paragraph can be found respectively on p. 31 (emphasis in the original); pp. 67–85 (which is an entire chapter entitled: I am the genius of myself); and p. 63.

213 Unger (2014).

214 Harré & Madden (In press); Harré, Madden, Brooks & Goodman (2017).

References

Acemoglu, D., & Robinson, J. A. (2013). *Why Nations Fail: The Origins of Power, Prosperity and Poverty*. London: Profile Books.

Albrecht, G. (2012). Psychoterratic conditions in a scientific and technological world. In P. H. Kahn, Jr. & P. H. Hasbach (Eds.), *Ecopsychology: Science, Totems, and the Technological Species* (pp. 241–264). Cambridge, MA: The MIT Press.

Allen, R. L. (2007). From *Black Awakening in Capitalist America*. In INCITE! Women of Color Against Violence (Ed.), *The Revolution Will Not Be Funded: Beyond the Non-profit Industrial Complex* (pp. 53–62). Cambridge, MA: South End Press.

Anderson, E. N. (2013). Culture and the wild. In P. H. Kahn, Jr. & P. H. Hasbach (Eds.), *The Rediscovery of the Wild* (pp. 157–180). Cambridge, MA: The MIT Press.

Armstrong, K. (2004). *The Spiral Staircase: My Climb Out of Darkness*. London, England: Harper Perennial.

Armstrong, K. (2006). *The Great Transformation: The Beginning of Our Religious Traditions*. New York, NY: Alfred A. Knopf.

Armstrong, K. (2010). *The Case for God: What Religion Really Means*. London, England: Vintage.

Bardel, M. H., Fontayne, P., Colombel, F., & Schiphof, L. (2010). Effects of match result and social comparison on sport state self-esteem fluctuations. *Psychology of Sport and Exercise, 11,* 171–176.

Becker, D. (2013). *One Nation Under Stress: The Trouble with Stress as an Idea*. New York, NY: Oxford University Press.

Berry, T. (1999). *The Great Work: Our Way into the Future*. New York, NY: Three Rivers Press.

Blackmore, E., Underhill, R., McQuilkin, J., Leach, R., & Holmes, T. (2013). *Common Cause for Nature: A Practical Guide to Values and Frames in Conservation*. Machynlleth, Wales: Public Interest Research Centre.

Bloch, C. (2002). Managing the emotions of competition and recognition in academia. *Sociological Review (50)*52, 113–131.

Block, P. (2008). *Community: The Structure of Belonging*. San Francisco, CA: Berrett-Koehler Publishers.

Blythe, C., Harré, N., Sharma, S., Dillon, V., Douglas, B., & Didsbury, A. (2013). Guiding principles for community engagement: Reflections on a school-based sustainability project. *Journal of Social Action in Counselling and Psychology, 5*(3), 44–69.

Brown, K. W., & Kasser, T. (2005). Are psychological and ecological well-being compatible? The role of values, mindfulness, and lifestyle. *Social Indicators Research, 74,* 349–368.

Campbell, D. T. (1976). *Assessing the Impact of Planned Social Change*. Hanover, NH: The Public Affairs Center, Dartmouth College.

Campbell, J. (1972). *Myths to Live By*. New York, NY: Penguin Compass.

Capra, F., & Luisi, P. L. (2014). *The Systems View of Life: A Unifying Vision*. Cambridge, England: Cambridge University Press.

Carse, J. P. (1986). *Finite and Infinite Games: A Vision of Life as Play and Possibility*. New York, NY: The Free Press.

Carse, J. P. (1994). *Breakfast at the Victory: The Mysticism of Ordinary Experience*. New York, NY: HarperOne.

Carse, J. P. (2008). *The Religious Case Against Belief*. New York, NY: Penguin.

Cavanaugh, W. T. (2008). *Being Consumed: Economics and Christian Desire*. Grand Rapids, MI: Wm. B. Eerdmans.

Chenoweth, E., & Stephan, M. J. (2011). *Why Civil Resistance Works: The Strategic Logic of Nonviolent Conflict*. New York, NY: Columbia University Press.

Clance, P. R., & Imes, S. (1978). The imposter phenomenon in high achieving women: Dynamics and therapeutic intervention. *Psychotherapy: Theory, Research, and Practice, 15*(3), 1–8.

Clayton, A. M. H., & Radcliffe, N. J. (1996). *Sustainability: A Systems Approach*. London, England: Earthscan.

Csikszentmihalyi, M. (1975). *Beyond Boredom and Anxiety*. San Francisco, CA: Jossey-Bass.

Davis, W. (2012). Sacred geography. In P. H. Kahn, Jr. & P. H. Hasbach (Eds.), *Ecopsychology: Science, Totems, and the Technological Species* (pp. 285–308). Cambridge, MA: The MIT Press.

de Almeida, A. F. J. (2007). Radical social change: Searching for a new foundation. In INCITE! Women of Color Against Violence (Ed.), *The Revolution Will Not Be Funded: Beyond the Non-profit Industrial Complex* (pp. 185–196). Cambridge, MA: South End Press.

de Botton, A. (2002). *The Art of Travel*. London, England: Penguin.

de Botton, A. (2012). *Religion for Atheists: A Non-believer's Guide to the Uses of Religions*. London, England: Hamish Hamilton.

De Koven, B. (1978/2013). *The Well-Played Game: A Player's Philosophy*. Cambridge, MA: The MIT Press.

de Waal, F. B. M. (2009). *The Age of Empathy: Nature's Lessons for a Kinder Society*. New York, NY: Harmony Books.

Diamond, J. (2005). *Collapse: How Societies Choose to Fail or Survive*. Camberwell, England: Allen Lane.

Dicker, P. (2009). The earth's subtle body: Recovering the poetry of the natural world. In J. Marshall (Ed.), *Depth Psychology, Disorder and Climate Change* (pp. 43–70). Sydney, Australia: Jung Downunder Books.

Douglass, J. W. (2008). *JFK and the Unspeakable: Why He Died and Why it Matters*. New York, NY: Touchstone.

Ehrlich, P. R. (2002). Human natures, nature conservation, and environmental ethics. *BioScience, 52*(1), 31–43.

Eisenstein, C. (2011). *Sacred Economics: Money, Gift and Society in the Age of Transition*. Berkeley, CA: Evolver Editions.

Eisenstein, C. (2016). Big problems need small solutions. *Resurgence and Ecologist 297,* 29–31.

Erikson, E. H. (1950). *Childhood and Society*. New York, NY: W. W. Norton & Co.

Fang, F. C., & Casadevall, A. (2015). Competitive science: Is competition ruining science? *Infection and Immunity, 83*, 1229–1233. https://doi.org/10.1128/IAI.02939-14.

Fisher, A. (2002). *Radical Ecopsychology: Psychology in the Service of Life*. Albany, NY: State University of New York Press.

Foale, S., Cohen, P., Januchowski-Hartley, S., Wenger, A., & Macintyre, M. (2011). Tenure and taboos: Origins and implications for fisheries in the Pacific. *Fish and Fisheries, 12*, 357–369.

Foreman, D. (2013). Five feathers for the cannot club. In P. H. Kahn, Jr. & P. H. Hasbach (Eds.), *The Rediscovery of the Wild* (pp. 181–206). Cambridge, MA: The MIT Press.

Fox, M. (1983). *Original Blessing*. New York, NY: Jeremy P. Tarcher/Putnam.

Freire, P. (1970/1996). *Pedagogy of the Oppressed*. London, England: Penguin Books.

Geering, L. (1994). *Tomorrow's God: How We Create Our Worlds*. Wellington, New Zealand: Bridget Williams Books.

Gilbert, E. (2006). *Eat, Pray, Love: One Woman's Search for Everything*. London, England: Bloomsbury.

Glick, P., & Fiske, S. T. (1996). The ambivalent sexism inventory: Differentiating hostile and benevolent sexism. *Journal of Personality and Social Psychology, 70*(3), 491–512. http://doi.org/10.1037/0022-3514.70.3.491

Gottlieb, R. S. (2006). *A Greener Faith: Religious Environmentalism and Our Planet's Future*. Oxford, England: Oxford University Press.

Graeber, D. (2013). *The Democracy Project*. London, England: Penguin Books.

Grant, B. M. (2016). *Critic and Conscience of the University: Animating the Infinite Game*. Paper presented at the Academic Identities Conference, Sydney.

Green, J. M. (1999). *Deep Democracy: Community, Diversity, and Transformation*. Lanham, MD: Rowan & Littlefield.

Grouzet, F. M. E., Ahuvia, A., Kim, Y., Ryan, R. M., Schumuck, P., Kasser, T., . . . Sheldon, K. M. (2005). The structure of goal contents across 15 cultures. *Jounal of Personality and Social Psychology, 89*(5), 800–816.

Haiven, M., & Khasnabish, A. (2014). *The Radical Imagination: Social Movement Research in the Age of Austerity*. Halifax & Winnipeg, Canada: Fernwood Publishing and London, England: Zed Books.

Hames, R. (2007). The ecologically noble savage debate. *Annual Review of Anthropology, 36*, 177–190.

Hamilton, C. (2008). *The Freedom Paradox: Towards a Post-secular Ethics*. Crows Nest, Australia: Allen & Unwin.

Hampden-Turner, C., & Trompenaars, F. (1997). *Mastering the Infinite Game: How Asian Values are Transforming Buiness Practices*. Oxford, England: Capstone.

Harré, N. (2018). *Psychology for a Better World: Working with People to Save the Planet*. Auckland, New Zealand: Auckland University Press.

Harré, N. (2013). Authentic leadership: Demonstrating and encouraging three ways of knowing. In D. Ladkin & C. Spiller (Eds.), *Authentic Leadership: Clashes, Convergences and Coalescences* (pp. 120–130). Oxford, England: Oxford University Press.

Harré, N., Bullen, P., & Olson, B. (2006). Storytelling: A workshop for inspiring group action. In R. M. McNair (Ed.), *Working for Peace: A Handbook for Practical Psychology and Other Tools* (pp. 116–120). Atascadero, CA: Impact.

Harré, N., Grant, B., Locke, K., & Sturm, S. (2017). The university as an infinite game: Revitalising activism in the academy. *Australian Universities' Review* 59(2), 5–13.

Harré, N., & Madden, H. (In press). The infinite game: A metaphor and workshop for living well together. *Ecopsychology*.

Harré, N., Madden, H., Brooks, R., & Goodman, J. (2017). Sharing values as a foundation for collective hope. *Journal of Social and Political Psychology*, 5(2), 342–366.

Harré, N., Tepavac, S., & Bullen, P. (2009). Integrity, efficacy and community in the stories of political activists. *Qualitative Research in Psychology*, 6(4), 330–345.

Hassan, Z. (2014). *The Social Labs Revolution: A New Approach to Solving Our Most Complex Challenges*. San Francisco, CA: Berrett-Koehler Publishers.

Hawe, P., Shiell, A., & Riley, T. (2009). Theorising interventions as events in systems. *American Journal of Community Psychology*, 43, 267–276.

Hawk, M. T. (2007). Native organizing before the non-profit industrial complex. In INCITE! Women of Color Against Violence (Ed.), *The Revolution Will Not Be Funded: Beyond the Non-profit Industrial Complex* (pp. 101–106). Cambridge, MA: South End Press.

Heffernan, M. (2014). *A Bigger Prize: Why Competition Isn't Everything and How We Do Better*. London, England: Simon & Schuster.

Hillman, J. (1989). *A Blue Fire: Selected Writings of James Hillman* (T. Moore, Ed.). New York, NY: Harper Perennial.

Hollan, D. (2012). Emerging issues in the cross-cultural study of empathy. *Emotion Review*, 4(1), 70–78.

Huizinga, J. (1950). *Homo Ludens: A Study of the Play-Element in Culture*. Boston, MA: The Beacon Press.

INCITE! Women of Color Against Violence. (2007). *The Revolution Will Not Be Funded: Beyond the Non-profit Industrial Complex*. Cambridge, MA: South End Press.

Jacobs, J. (1961). *The Death and Life of Great American Cities*. New York, NY: Vintage Books.

James, W. (1902). *The Varieties of Religious Experience: A Study in Human Nature*. Retrieved from http://www.gutenberg.org/ebooks/621

Jamieson, D. (2008). *Ethics and the Environment: An Introduction*. Cambridge, England: Cambridge University Press.

Janis, I. L. (1983). *Groupthink: Psychological Studies of Policy Decisions and Fiascoes* (2nd Edition). Boston, MA: Houghton Mifflin.

Kahane, A. (2012). *Transformative Scenario Planning: Working Together to Change the Future*. San Francisco, CA: Berrett-Koehler Publishers.

Kahn, Jr., P. H. (1997). Developmental psychology and the biophilia hypothesis: Children's affiliation with nature. *Developmental Review*, 17, 1–61.

Kahn, Jr., P. H. (2003). The development of environmental moral identity. In S. Clayton & S. Opotow (Eds.), *Identity and the Natural Environment: The Psychological Significance of Nature* (pp. 113–134). Cambridge, MA: The MIT Press.

Kahn, Jr., P. H., & Hasbach, P. II. (2012). Introduction. In P. H. Kahn, Jr. & P. H. Hasbach (Eds.), *Ecopsychology: Science, Totems, and the Technological Species* (pp. 1–22). Cambridge, MA: The MIT Press.

Kasser, T. (2011). *Values and Human Wellbeing*. The Bellagio Intitiative. Brighton, England: IDS. Retrieved from http://opendocs.ids.ac.uk/opendocs/handle/123456789/3721

Kasser, T., & Ryan, R. M. (1993). A dark side of the American dream: Correlates of financial success as a central life aspiration. *Journal of Personality and Social Psychology, 65*(2), 410–422.

Kellert, S. R., & Wilson, E. O. (Eds.) (2003). *The Biophilia Hypothesis*. Washington, DC: Island Press.

Kelly, S. M. (2010). *Coming Home: The Birth and Transformation of the Planetary Era*. Great Barrington, MA: Lindisfarne Books.

Kerr, J. H., Wilson, G. V., Bowling, A., & Sheahan, J. P. (2005). Game outcome and elite Japanese women's field hockey players' experience of emotions and stress. *Psychology of Sport and Exercise, 6*, 251–263.

Kets de Vries, M. F. R. (2014). Death and the executive: Encounters with the 'stealth' motivator. *Organizational Dynamics, 43*, 247–256.

Klein, N. (2014). *This Changes Everything: Capitalism vs. the Climate*. New York, NY: Simon & Schuster.

Ku, L., & Zaroff, C. (2014). How far is your money from your mouth? The effects of intrinsic relative to extrinsic values on willingness to pay and protect the environment. *Journal of Environmental Psychology, 40*, 472–483.

Kushner, T. (2004). Despair is a lie we tell ourselves. In P. R. Loeb (Ed.), *The Impossible Will Take a Little While: A Citizen's Guide to Hope in a Time of Fear* (pp. 201–203). New York, NY: Basic Books.

Leopold, A. (1949). *A Sand County Almanac*. New York: Oxford University Press.

Macey, J. (2007). *World as Lover, World as Self: Courage for Global Justice and Ecological Renewal*. Berkeley, CA: Parallax Press.

Marshall, J. (2009). Depth psychology and social innovation: The creative face of chaos. In J. Marshall (Ed.), *Depth Psychology, Disorder and Climate Change* (pp. 197–217). Sydney, Australia: Jung Downunder Books.

Maslow, A. H. (1970). *Motivation and Personality*. New York: Harper & Row.

McBride, T. (2009). Earth protector or earth destroyer. In J. Marshall (Ed.), *Depth Psychology, Disorder and Climate Change* (pp. 283–299). Sydney, Australia: Jung Downunder Books.

McGonigal, J. (2011). *Reality is Broken: Why Games Make Us Better and How They Can Change the World*. New York, NY: Penguin.

McIntosh, A. (2001/2004). *Soil and Soul: People versus Corporate Power*. London, England: Aurum Press.

McIntosh, A. (2012). *Rekindling Community: Connecting People, Environment and Spirituality*. Totnes, England: Green Books.

McIntosh, A., & Carmichael, M. (2016). *Spiritual Activism: Leadership as Service*. Cambridge, England: Green Books.

Merton, T. (1965/1979). *Love and Living*. Orlando, FL: Harcourt.

Merton, T. (2008). *Thomas Merton: A Life in Letters*. New York, NY: HarperOne.

Ministry for the Environment. (2015). *New Zealand's Climate Change Target*. Wellington: New Zealand Government.

Monbiot, G. (2013). *Feral: Searching for Enchantment on the Frontiers of Rewilding*. London, England: Allen Lane.

Murphy, S. (2012). *Minding the Earth: Mending the World*. Sydney, Australia: Picador.

Myers, O. E. (2007). *The Significance of Children and Animals: Social Development and Our Connections to Other Species*. West Lafayette, IN: Purdue University Press.

Myers, O. E., & Saunders, C. D. (2002). Animals as links toward developing caring relationships with the natural world. In P. H. Kahn, Jr. & S. R. Kellert (Eds.), *Children and Nature: Psychological, Sociocultural, and Evolutionary Investigations* (pp. 153–176). Cambridge, MA: The MIT Press.

Naess, A. (2008). *The Ecology of Wisdom*. Berkeley: Counterpoint.

Nakamura, J., & Csikszentmihalyi, M. (2002). The concept of flow. In C. R. Snyder & S. J. Lopez (Eds.), *Handbook of Positive Psychology* (pp. 89–105). Oxford, England: Oxford University Press.

Noonan, A., & Macken, J. (2009). Stardust. In J. Marshall (Ed.), *Depth Psychology, Disorder and Climate Change* (pp. 219–236). Sydney: Jung Downunder Books.

Nowak, M. (2011). *Super Cooperators: Evolution, Altruism and Human Behaviour*. Edinburgh, Scotland: Canongate.

Nucci, L. (2001). *Education in the Moral Domain*. Cambridge, England: Cambridge University Press.

Olson, E. E., & Eoyang, G. H. (2001). *Facilitating Organization Change: Lessons From Complexity Science*. San Francisco, CA: Jossey-Bass/Pfeiffer.

Piff, P. K., Kraus, M. W., Côté, S., Cheng, B. H., & Keltner, D. (2010). Having less, giving more: The influence of social class on prosocial behavior. *Interpersonal Relations and Group Processes, 99*(5), 771–784.

Pirsig, R. M. (1974). *Zen and the Art of Motorcycle Maintenance: An Inquiry into Values*. London, England: Corgi.

Plotkin, B. (2003). *Soulcraft: Crossing Into the Mysteries of Nature and the Psyche*. Novato, CA: New World Library.

Plotkin, B. (2008). *Nature and the Human Soul: Cultivating Wholeness and Community in a Fragmented World*. Navato, CA: New World Library.

Pollan, M. (2006). *The Omnivore's Dilemma: A Natural History of Four Meals*. London, England: Bloomsbury.

Pope Francis. (2015). Encyclical Letter of the Holy Father Francis on Care for Our Common Home. Retrieved from http://w2.vatican.va/content/francesco/en/encyclicals/documents/papa-francesco_20150524_enciclica-laudato-si.html

Randall, R. (2009). Loss and climate change: The cost of parallel narratives. *Ecopsychology, 1*(1), 118–129.

Rivlin, G. (2016). *Rigged: Supermarket Shelves for Sale*. Washington: Center for Science in the Public Interest.Retrieved from https://cspinet.org/sites/default/files/attachment/Rigged%20report_0.pdf

Rodríguez, D. (2007). The political logic of the non-profit industrial complex. In INCITE! Women of Color Against Violence (Ed.), *The Revolution Will Not Be Funded: Beyond the Non-profit Industrial Complex* (pp. 21–40). Cambridge, MA: South End Press.

Rojas, P. X. (2007). Are the cops in our heads and hearts? In INCITE! Women of Color Against Violence (Ed.), *The Revolution Will Not Be Funded: Beyond the Non-profit Industrial Complex* (pp. 197–214). Cambridge, MA: South End Press.

Rønnow, T. (2006). *Saving Nature: Religion as Environmentalism, Environmentalism as Religion* (Vol. 4). Berlin, Germany: LIT.

Russell, B. (1930). *The Conquest of Happiness*. New York: Liveright Publishing.

Ryan, R. M., & Deci, E. L. (2000). Self-determination theory and the facilitation of intrinsic motivation, social development, and well-being. *American Psychologist, 55*(1), 68–78.

Ryan, R. M., & Deci, E. L. (2002). An overview of self-determination theory: An organismic-dialetical perspective. In E. L. Deci & R. M. Ryan (Eds.), *Handbook of Self-Determination Research* (pp. 3–36). Rochester, NY: University of Rochester Press.

Sahlberg, P. (2015). *Finnish Lessons: What Can the World Learn from Educational Change in Finland* (2nd Edition). New York, NY: Teachers College Press.

Samuel, L. R. (2010). *Freud on Madison Avenue: Motivational Research and Subliminal Advertising in America*. Philadelphia, PA: University of Pennsylvania Press.

Sato, I. (1988). Bosozoku: Flow in Japanese motorcycle gangs. In M. Csikszentmihalyi & I. S. Csikszentimihalyi (Eds.), *Optimal Experience: Psychological Studies of Flow in Consciousness* (pp. 92–117). Cambridge, England: Cambridge University Press.

Sayre, N. F. (2012). The politics of the anthropogenic. *Annual Review of Anthropology, 41*, 57–70.

Schumacher, E. F. (1973). *Small is Beautiful: A Study of Economics as if People Mattered*. New York, NY: Harper Perennial.

Sewall, L. (2012). Beauty and the brain. In P. H. Kahn, Jr. & P. H. Hasbach (Eds.), *Ecopsychology: Science, Totems, and the Technological Species* (pp. 265–284). Cambridge, MA: The MIT Press.

Sheldon, K. M., & McGregor, H. A. (2000). Extrinsic value orientation and 'the tragedy of the commons'. *Journal of Personality, 68*(2), 383–411.

Sheldrake, R. (2013). *The Science Delusion: Freeing the Spirit of Enquiry*. London, England: Coronet.

Smith, A. (2007). Introduction. In INCITE! Women of Color Against Violence (Ed.), *The Revolution Will Not Be Funded: Beyond the Non-profit Industrial Complex* (pp. 1–18). Cambridge, MA: South End Press.

Stacey, R. D. (1996). *Complexity and Creativity in Organizations*. San Francisco, CA: Berrett-Koehler Publishers.

Starhawk. (2002). *Webs of Power: Notes from the Global Uprising*. Gabriola Island, Canada: New Society Publishers.

Stengers, I., Despret, V., & Collective. (2014). *Women Who Make a Fuss: The Unfaithful Daughters of Virginia Woolf*. Minneapolis, MN: Univocal.

Stucke, M. E. (2013). Is competition always good? *Journal of Antitrust Enforcement, 1*(1), 162–197.

Stutchbury, B. (2013). Wild wings. In P. H. Kahn, Jr. & P. H. Hasbach (Eds.), *The Rediscovery of the Wild* (pp. 71–91). Cambridge, MA: The MIT Press.

Tacey, D. (2009a). Entering the dream of nature: James Hillman, Australian poetry and Aboriginal dreaming. In J. Marshall (Ed.), *Depth Psychology, Disorder and Climate Change* (pp. 365–394). Sydney, Australia: Jung Downunder Books.

Tacey, D. (2009b). The sacred from below: The ecological spirit of our time. In J. Marshall (Ed.), *Depth Psychology, Disorder and Climate Change* (pp. 265–276). Sydney, Australia: Jung Downunder Books.

Taleb, N. N. (2012). *Antifragile: Things that Gain from Disorder*. London, England: Penguin.

Taylor, B. (2010). *Dark Green Religion: Nature Spirituality and the Planetary Future*. Berkeley, CA: University of California Press.

Taylor, B. (2011). Earth and nature-based spirituality (Part 1): From deep ecology to radical environmentalism. *Religion, 31*(2), 175–193.

Taylor, M. C. (2007). *After God*. Chicago, IL: The University of Chicago Press.

Thomas, E. M. (2003). The lion/Bushman relationship in Nyae Nyae in the 1950s: A relationship crafted in the old way. *Anthropologica, 45*(1), 73–78.

Townrow, C., Laurence, N., Blythe, C., Long, J., & Harré, N. (2016). The Maui's dolphin challenge: Lessons from a school-based litter reduction project. *Australasian Journal of Environmental Education, 32*(3), 288–308.

Tudge, C. (2013). *Why Genes are Not Selfish and People are Nice*. Edinburgh, Scotland: Floris Books.

Turiel, E. (2002). *The Culture of Morality: Social Development, Context, and Conflict*. Cambridge, England: Cambridge University Press.

Turner, C. (2007). *The Geography of Hope: A Tour of the World We Need*. Toronto, Canada: Vintage Canada.

Unger, R. M. (Writer) & D. Edmonds & N. Warburton (Directors). (2014). *Roberto Unger on What is Wrong with the Social Sciences Today?* Social Science Bites: Sage. Retrieved from www.socialsciencebites.com

van Egmond, K. (2014). *Sustainable Civilization*. London, England: Palgrave Macmillan.

Vickers, G. (1965/1995). *The Art of Judgment: A Study of Policy Making*. Thousand Oaks, CA: Sage.

Wilbur, K. (2001). *A Theory of Everything: An Integral Vision for Business, Politics, Science, and Spirituality*. Boston, MA: Shambala.

Wilson, G. V., & Kerr, J. H. (1999). Affective responses to success and failure: A study of winning and losing in competitive rugby. *Personality and Individual Differences, 27*, 85–99.

Woodman, C. (2011). *Unfair Trade: The Shocking Truth Behind 'Ethical' Business*. London, England: Random House Business Books.

Yeates, J. A. M., & Lehman, N. (2016). RNA networks at the origins of life. *Biochemical Society, 38*(2), 8–12.

Internet materials

After atheism: New perspectives on God and religion, part 4 – James P. Carse. (2004, July 8). Retrieved from http://www.cbc.ca/radio/ideas/after-atheism-new-perspectives-on-god-and-religion-part-4-1.2914009

Because the computer says so. (2015, June 14). Retrieved from http://www.nzherald.co.nz/nz/news/article.cfm?c_id=1&objectid=11464802

Bristol's traumatic last hanging and the Gaol's closure. (2001, September 20). Retrieved from http://www.bbc.co.uk/bristol/content/features/2001/09/20/new-gaol/new-gaol4.shtml

Confronting Empire – Arundhati Roy. (2003, January 30). Retrieved from
http://www.outlookindia.com/website/story/confronting-empire/218738
Denmark second | Denmark Trumps the Netherlands at being no. 2.
(2017, February 2). Retrieved from https://www.youtube.com/
watch?v=ryppmnDbqJY
Ecosystems & wildlife under threat. Retrieved from http://wwf.panda.org/
what_we_do/footprint/agriculture/soy/ecosystems/ (accessed 4 July 2017).
Execution of Sarah Harriet Thomas at Bristol. Retrieved from http://trove.nla.
gov.au/newspaper/article/62045132 (accessed 4 July 2017).
Exploring how and why trees 'talk' to each other – Suzanne Simard.
(2016, September 1). Retrieved from http://e360.yale.edu/feature/
exploring_how_and_why_trees_talk_to_each_other/3029/
Global dairy industry 'mooooving' forward. Retrieved from http://www.
stats.govt.nz/browse_for_stats/snapshots-of-nz/yearbook/environment/
agriculture/dairy.aspx (accessed 4 July 2017).
Global palm oil demand fuelling deforestation. Retrieved from http://www.
worldwatch.org/node/6059 (accessed 4 July 2017).
Household economic survey: Year ended June 2013. (2013, November 28).
Retrieved from http://www.stats.govt.nz/browse_for_stats/people_and_
communities/Households/HouseholdEconomicSurvey_HOTPYeJun13/
Commentary.aspx
Humans have ten times more bacteria than human cells: How do microbial
communities affect human health? (2008, June 5). Retrieved from http://
www.sciencedaily.com/releases/2008/06/080603085914.htm
Kate McKenzie now only woman CEO in NZX50. (2017, February 21).
Retrieved from http://www.nzherald.co.nz/business/news/article.
cfm?c_id=3&objectid=11804694
Key world energy statistics, 2017. Retrieved from http://www.iea.org/
publications/freepublications/keyword2017 (accessed 26 October 2017).
New Zealand's 2030 climate change target. (2016, December 20). Retrieved
from http://www.mfe.govt.nz/climate-change/reducing-greenhouse-gas-
emissions/new-zealand%E2%80%99s-post-2020-climate-change-target
New Zealand's greenhouse gas inventory 1990–2013. (2015, April). Retrieved
from http://www.mfe.govt.nz/sites/default/files/media/Climate%20Change/
nz-greenhouse-gas-inventory-snapshot-2015.pdf
Our duty to the earth. (2009, March 26). Retrieved from https://www.
theguardian.com/commentisfree/belief/2009/mar/26/religion-anglicanism
Paxman vs Russell Brand. (2013, October 23). Retrieved from https://www.
youtube.com/watch?v=3YR4CseY9pk
Playing the game of life – Alan Watts. (2013, December 11). Retrieved from
https://www.youtube.com/watch?v=QXvoYGrnuv8
Remarks at a luncheon for gubernatorial candidate Bill Simon in Stockton. (2002,
August 23). Retrieved from http://www.presidency.ucsb.edu/ws/?pid=64884
Russel Brand destroys MSNBC talk show host. (2013, June 19). Retrieved from
https://www.youtube.com/watch?v=ynUjo99Gzbk
The 6 killer apps of prosperity – Niall Ferguson. (2011, July). Retrieved from
http://www.ted.com/talks/niall_ferguson_the_6_killer_apps_of_
prosperity?language=en

The Netherlands welcomes Trump in his own words. (2017, January 23).
Retrieved from https://www.youtube.com/watch?v=ELD2AwFN9Nc

The STM Report: An overview of scientific and scholarly journal publishing.
(2012, November). Retrieved from http://www.stm-assoc.org/2012_12_11_
STM_Report_2012.pdf

The world in 2050: When the 5 largest economies are the BRICs and US.
(2012, February 17). Retrieved from http://www.theatlantic.com/business/
archive/2012/02/the-world-in-2050-when-the-5-largest-economies-are-the-
brics-and-us/253160/

The world: Life expectancy (2050) – Top 100+. Retrieved from http://www.geoba.
se/population.php?pc=world&type=015&year=2050&st=rank&asde=&page=1

The world's richest and poorest countries. (2017, February 13). Retrieved
from https://www.gfmag.com/global-data/economic-data/
worlds-richest-and-poorest-countries

To believe is human; to doubt, divine – Peter Rollins. (2013, November 11).
Retrieved from https://www.youtube.com/watch?v=hzkwj7bUvUY

Western Springs College Waste Minimisation Report. (2013, March). Retrieved
from http://www.westernsprings.school.nz/WesternSpringsCollege_
NewsStories/WSC_Waste_Wise_Report_2013.pdf

What to expect from Weight Watchers meetings. Retrieved from http://diet.love-
toknow.com/wiki/Weight_Watchers_Meetings#LRHmdCm2yqqW0j8b.97
(accessed 4 July 2017).

World population to reach 9.7 billion by 2050 new study predicts. (2013, October
2). Retrieved from http://www.telegraph.co.uk/news/earth/10348822/World-
population-to-reach-9.7-billion-by-2050-new-study-predicts.html

Acknowledgments

This book has taken many years, from when I first heard James P. Carse interviewed on the CBC Radio podcast *Ideas*, through to its publication. The Infinite Game workshops grew alongside the book, so I would first like to thank all the organisations that invited me to run a workshop or to give a talk, and the participants in those workshops and talks. I have learnt so much from all of you and your insights appear throughout the book. In particular, Idil Gaziulusoy helped design the first workshops; and Hannah Mitchell, Kim Elliott and Edwin Monk-Fromont were also early enthusiasts. It was Dan Ducker, who, when I talked with him about the idea of the infinite game being an actual game, suggested people write their own cards. This led to the values exercise which is a centre point to both the workshop and the book. Nalini Singh has helped run workshops and added considerable flair and intellectual insight.

Rachel Brown and the other staff at the Sustainable Business Network invited me to deliver a number of Infinite Game talks and an Authentic Leadership course that was based on the infinite game. Doris Zuur and others from Orientation Aotearoa also provided more than their share of Infinite Game opportunities, as has the Sustainable Schools team at Auckland Council – in particular Cate Jessep and Bridget Glasgow. Thea Kilian – thank you, too, for the opportunities you've provided to share the game with teachers and students. Several colleagues at the University of Auckland have also attended games, or organised for me to run workshops with their classes. I'd like to thank Lesley Stone, Charlotte Blythe, James Russell, Fabiana Kubke, Ross McDonald, and the facilitators of Science Scholars in particular.

In 2014 my sister Laila Harré and I did a 'Rethink the System' tour of the North Island, and held 28 meetings. At each of these we did a mini Infinite Game, so I would like to thank all our hosts, and everyone we met on that amazing journey. I'd also like to thank Laila herself, my inspirational, dedicated sister who is an infinite player extraordinaire.

I've had so many conversations outside these settings, and they've all refined my ideas. People who I've discussed the infinite game with on numerous occasions and whose wisdom I've undoubtedly appropriated include Manuel Riemer, Charlotte Blythe, Ivan Harré, Elizabeth Fahey, Francisco Barros, Viviana Becker and Rod Oram. My Transition Town friends have also attended workshops, discussed concepts, and generally keep reminding me of how it is possible to live with joy, love, and a drive to improve the world. Two other networks that keep infinite play alive for me are the Western Springs College Sustainability Panel and the Faculty of Science Sustainability Network at the University of Auckland. Thanks, too, to everyone who sent me feedback in response to my Infinite Game blog.

I've worked with several colleagues on variations of the Infinite Game workshop and related academic publications. Helen Madden, in particular, has spent many hours working on the values data, co-written two articles, and been a great personal support during the infinite game process. Rowan Brooks has also been integral to the data analysis, and helped my thinking on the potential of this metaphor for activism. Barbara Grant, Kirsten Locke, Sean Sturm, Stephen Turner and Anna Boswell have helped apply the infinite game to the university and been a great source of ideas and support. Thanks to Jonathan Goodman for the construction of the word clouds. Ties Coomber, Hannah Green, Blake Steele and Leon Russell have also done research using the infinite game metaphor and Ties and I have had many discussions about its applications.

People who have helped with the writing in particular include Judy Wilford, Geoff Walker, and my informal writing buddies – Max Harré, Fran Harré and Clare Feeney. Tom Styak and Cassandra Chapman gave me careful feedback on early drafts. Thanks to Laila Harré, John Harré, and Max Harré for your proofreading and suggestions. Thanks to Max Thomas for setting up the book's website.

Thank you to Sam Elworthy and the team at Auckland University Press for your support and faith in this book. Thanks also to Mike Wagg for meticulous editing, Amy Tansell for typesetting, and Nicola Makiri van Aardt for proofreading.

My family have been an integral part of making this book happen. Keith, I've worked through most of these ideas with you and you've kept the home fires burning when I've been distracted with getting the book done. My father, children and siblings have also taken an interest in, and supported me through, this project – thank you all.

Niki Harré
November 2017